Thinking Strategy
and a reappraisal of planning

Thinking Strategy
and a reappraisal of planning

by Ian Webb

The Industrial Society

First published 1989 by
The Industrial Society
Peter Runge House
3 Carlton House Terrace
London SW1Y 5DG
Telephone 01 839 4300

© *The Industrial Society*, 1989

ISBN 0 85290 454 1

British Library Cataloguing in Publication Data
Webb, Ian
    Thinking Strategy and a reappraisal of planning.
    1. Business firms planning
    I. Title
    658.4'012

Typeset by Ace Filmsetting Limited, Frome, Somerset
Printed and bound in Great Britain by Biddles Limited, Guildford, Surrey

Contents

ix

Foreword

All organisations must look to the future. With the advent of 1992 and in the face of increasing competition, no company can be without a framework within which to develop their business in the years ahead. *Thinking Strategy* is one such framework, and this book will guide the reader through the important aspects of this complex subject.

There is, of course, no magic formula for corporate success. Strategy and planning are just two key areas of a corporate development plan that should include people as well as products, management training as well as market forecasting. *Thinking Strategy* will help the reader to isolate a unique strategy suitable for their organisation and in doing so, focus on the competititve edge they will need in a national or international market place.

Alistair Graham
Director

Preface

In setting out to write this book, I wanted a work which would be consistent with every corporate situation I have come across and which would attempt to encourage the reader to start on the path towards a strategy of his or her own. The organisations I have worked in, or for, now make a long list—well into three figures in fact—and most of them have approached, or appeared to approach, strategic issues with their own styles. Perspectives on corporate appraisal and strategy have differed, depending on whether the viewpoint was from the City and financial markets, from within an organisation, or from an academic institution or consultancy. No one was necessarily wrong; all could simply have followed alternative routes up the same mountain. However, the increasing sense of complication, the further I researched strategy, justified yet another attempt at a summary.

Of the outstanding issues around the subject, by far the most prominent were the need to assess the relationship of planning to strategy and to identify the contribution of planning. As a former enthusiast for the ideas of number-crunching, planning and determinism, having been through a phase of partial disillusionment, my interest was revived, in 1986, by a project on management development funded by the Manpower Services Commission and involving 40 companies. Among the findings of this project was that the greatest and most effective efforts in training and management education are strongly associated with participative planning systems. Unexpected at the time, this finding is, of course, very similar to one of Likert's in the early 1960s; that is, that participation leads to corporate effectiveness. A close connection between management development and progress seemed an entirely reasonable assumption. Participation, through planning, was seen to have valuable consequences and additional, wider effects. So despite the mixed reports on planning down the years, it had to be made to work.

I am particularly grateful to Sir Raymond Lygo of British Aerospace, Andrew Lamont of De Beers, Tony Vicars-Miles of Shell and Peter Curry of Unitech, who gave interviews on their companies; confidently setting the direction on several crucial issues. Since seeing them, important developments include British Aerospace completing its acquisition of Rover Group, Minorco bidding for Consolidated Gold Fields and Unitech selling a major equity stake to a Swiss concern and then making a large US acquisition which also brought a Japanese interest.

Many associations are reflected in the book in some way and I would like to acknowledge conversations on strategy, early in the investigation, with Olli Eloranta of Toimialaconsultit, Helsinki, and with Brian Taylor of Wardle Storeys. These sparked off a number of ideas which helped to develop the work. But above all, I must thank my wife, Sue, for her encouragement and painstaking review of the penultimate draft, which is now much more friendly to the reader than it was before.

Ian Webb
February 1989

Introduction

"Strategy" is a term which is in danger of being overworked. It is used for a variety of purposes in commerce, and often its meaning is obscure. Usually it conveys a sense of forward movement, of ongoing progress for the organisation concerned. It is found in connection with several disciplines—for instance, production strategy, marketing strategy, personnel strategy—and sometimes it enhances a lowly function. Definitions abound, with varying emphasis on management, direction, leadership and resource allocation.

Strategy can also be defined in terms of the functions often required to carry it out. "Corporate planning" suddenly became known as "strategic planning". Likewise, "corporate planners" changed their name to "strategic planners" and from there it was a small step to define strategy as the corporate plan itself. This was, after all, a tangible result from a process normally started through an intention to produce a strategy. Somehow one pictures a weighty document, in the name of "The Strategy", being delivered, with a roll of drums worthy of King Herod, to the board room table, whereupon the planning manager receives a vote of thanks for the several man-years of time it represents.

DEFINITION OF STRATEGY AND TACTICS

So there is scope for confusion over what a strategy is and what it covers. In this book, it is defined as *the process of deciding a future course*

1

for a business and so organising and steering that business as to attempt to bring about that future course. Typically, strategy will involve thinking far ahead, but this need not necessarily be the case. Thus, the organisational strategist may be seen as being like a traveller on a winding road to an unknown though worthwhile destination, negotiating hazards and bends as they are presented. In this example, his or her only pre-defined objectives need be some strategic guidelines, such as a concern for quality and an earnings growth target.

Strategy frequently involves certain distinct aspects of coordinating and running a business. Although such matters are not strictly part of a strategy, it is misleading to consider commercial, strategic issues in complete isolation. So while mission statements, goals, resource allocation, plans, tactics, reviews and all the rest, need not necessarily be part of a strategy, normally most of them will be.

Within any strategic programme there will be certain actions and steps of limited scope and duration which contribute to the overall picture; these may be distinguished as "tactics". Although in practice the distinction is normally subjective, *tactical issues tend to apply over the near and medium terms and address just a part of activities.* Strategic issues, by contrast, will be of broader scope and longer duration. But perspectives differ according to organisational levels; what appears at the bottom as a strategy may be seen from the top as just a tactical matter. By this definition, most of what is usually called "strategic" is really "tactical", however, the two terms are largely interchangeable.

Despite being a fashionable topic at the moment, strategy has had mixed reviews in recent years. There have been disappointments, misunderstandings and unrealised hopes as businesses have searched by trial and error for procedures which work. So the value of the concept has been questioned. However, compared with the situation two decades ago, many pitfalls are now recognised and a clearer impression of the subject can be given. A more stable picture has emerged, and so it is time for a reappraisal.

THE ILLUSTRATIVE COMPANIES

For this book four companies have been chosen to illustrate contrasting aspects of the strategic problems: British Aerospace PLC, De Beers Consolidated Mines Ltd., Shell UK Ltd. and Unitech PLC.

British Aerospace

Perhaps the outstanding strategic challenge in UK manufacturing today, British Aerospace was formed in the mid-1970s with the nationalisation of all the major producers of fixed wing aircraft not already in public ownership. Four years later, the Thatcher Administration indicated its intention to privatise the company, and early in 1981 British Aerospace became the first major corporation to be resold to the private sector. Subsequently, there have been major acquisitions. This evolving pattern has seen great changes in strategy, structure and corporate culture, while the group's diversification, innovation and style of direction demonstrate the interaction between strategy and incoming opportunities.

De Beers Consolidated Mines

Some strategic issues are illustrated more easily in retrospect and in its centenary year, De Beers is an excellent example of this. With a very well documented history, the company has for the greater part of the time generated outstanding competitive advantage. Furthermore, it demonstrates some points more clearly in that it lacks most of the complications of multiple products and markets. Its group is also of interest to a study of strategy, as it is one of the very few companies of world stature with a base outside the triad areas of Europe, North America and Japan.

Shell UK

Part of the Royal Dutch Shell Group, one of the world's largest and best known corporations, Shell has been at the forefront of developing and using corporate planning techniques for over a quarter of a century. Its experience of using the method in a large and complicated organisation is thus second to none, and invaluable in attempting to reappraise its use within the overall context of strategy.

Unitech

Founded in 1962, Unitech is a distributor and manufacturer of electronic components, subassemblies and ancillary equipment. Today, thanks to a combination of rapid organic growth and acquisitions, it is an outstanding example of a small business which grew into a major group. Its diversification, structure and style of operation have been set, or influenced, very closely through strategy. Unitech's pattern—of a small group in the centre controlling subsidiaries—is a prime example of an expanding high technology company with a low, flat structure.

1
Surviving without a formal strategy

The definitions adopted in this book for "strategy" and "tactics" are sufficiently broad that most organisations have something of both of these already. However, it is quite possible to decide the future course of a business, and to organise and steer it accordingly, without ever formalising the strategic process. Even where it is formalised, the strategist may instinctively go about his or her business taking decisions which would only be termed "strategic" by an outsider. Informal approaches to strategy are widespread. Some organisations appear to have no strategy at all, except, possibly in the minds of their leaders. Others may lack some attributes of strategy such as planning, yet manage to position themselves in an information flow so that a successful course is chosen. Still others somehow manage to translate a collection of hopes, customs, traditions and commercial principles into action.

SOME DANGERS OF HAVING A STRATEGY

Moreover, such an informal state as described above may be vastly preferable to some of the dangers which can be introduced by a formal strategy. Inadequate or incorrect analyses, policies and tactics—poorly conceived from the available information and badly coordinated—may all be worse than simply doing nothing. Above all, perhaps, are the dangers of an inflexible approach. Though a strategy may have represented the best possible view when first outlined, it can become outmoded and need revision, without which it gradually becomes an adverse influence.

Neglect of a formal strategy can arise for either personal or structural reasons, and the problem can be complicated by the lack of clear signals showing whether or not a strategic programme is on course. If it is just a matter of registering gain or loss after a specified short time, there should be no problem. But the long time-scales usually involved in a strategy and the high degree of subjective assessment required for many of its aspects make such an easy solution quite unattainable. Part of the answer is to have a periodic and frequent review, conducted by people who really want the strategy to work and who are flexible in their views. However, some ideas are much easier to alter than others; speculative opinions, in particular, can be a personal matter which, once decided, are hard to change.

Such conditions are often seen in smaller companies, where the single-mindedness and determination of the proprietor are key qualities during the first few years after a start-up—to the extent that had he or she been open to too much criticism, the business might never have started. But as the company broadens out, some different criteria come into play and the proprietor's early entrepreneurial qualities and fixed set of goals may not be quite appropriate.

SOME INFORMAL APPROACHES TO STRATEGY

It is quite possible therefore for circumstances to make a strategy by default the best solution. Even where a formal strategy exists, many matters may be covered informally. Usually, in such cases, there is an aspect of corporate culture or philosophy which happens to coincide with some of the fundamental requirements of the business. Virtually any part of a strategy can be handled in such a way. For example, a retailer might have run an organisation for several generations on the principle of "Buy in the cheapest market, stack the goods high and make sure you are not under-priced by anyone". Provided the business is at the volume end of the market and in one of just a few categories of goods, such a principle—with low costs as a tactic— might have guided it for decades. Had the market niche altered, or had there been some other change, such as a technical discontinuity, this principle alone might well have been insufficient, although it might still have provided a base to which other tactics could have been added.

Similarly, it is possible to be competing on quality for reasons which have nothing to do with a conscious strategy. Statements such as "The founder of this business, so many generations ago, established the principle that our workmanship shall be second to none", can guide an organisation for years. Once again, a stable market is likely to be a crucial, though feasible, assumption. Stable markets may be in a minority but they are not all that difficult to find.

Technical change is less easy to handle informally, but it is still possible. Combine a measure of ignorance with a passion for the most modern equipment and an active enthusiasm for the latest techniques and what happens? Under conditions of rapid technical development and change, the operational functions can be kept ahead without any other strategic intention to stay competitive. Naturally, this approach is open to grave mistakes. It is this style of thinking which led to some companies spending a small fortune on mainframe computers which then lay virtually idle for a few years. And where change is relatively slow, it is possible to build a new plant and find that its full costs are not the lowest in the sector. However, in the right place and at the right time, technical change can be managed in such an informal manner.

Of the readily observed examples of a strategic process operating as if by default, perhaps the richest field is among human resources. Where the quality of staff is by far the most important fundamental, questions of selection and motivation can dominate other strategic issues. In many service industries, professional firms and even some manufacturing activities, certain personnel traditions, customs and rules of thumb overshadow everything else. Merely attracting and selecting good staff can be enough. Keeping them virtually assures success. Some strategic attention to the organisational structure might improve the position still further, but if people really matter, other mistakes can be carried by a successful human resources policy.

SOME CHARACTERISTICS OF ORGANISATIONS WITH INFORMAL STRATEGIES

In cases where informal strategy has guided a business to fame and fortune right through from the nineteenth century, commercial life can seem all too easy at first sight. Closer observation, however, may reveal that this is not a pattern to be copied directly. Many of the medium-sized examples without either a formal strategy, or any clear, visible, guiding principle, may be found to have substantial assets. These may be used inefficiently, but they lower the cost base and overall risk profile so that survival is possible despite amateur management methods.

In other examples, a limited range of strategic options may be seen, with one having paramount importance. Structure tends to be simple and the information needs are limited. Size is thus likely to be small, and with the proprietor the sole source of direction some incipient difficulties over coordinating the business are forestalled. Were activities to be expanded the problems would soon surface, which is one reason why many small businesses are destined to remain small.

Perhaps the outstanding case against running a company with an informal strategy, is that many are found to be ill-prepared for innovation and change. Where a virtue is made of post-rationalising success back to the genius and vision of the founder, it may be inferred that once there was a strategy—and doubtless an excellent one. The effects of such a leader can linger on for decades through the corporate philosophy, structure, pattern of business and even key appointments. Events can be fortuitous in these situations and frequently, they prosper for many years before finally losing their independence, but most major companies choose a more active style of direction.

2
Business strategy and the military example

Another reason why long-established corporations have managed for years without thinking about a "strategy" as such, is that the term has only recently been applied to commerce. Modern use of strategy appears to go back to the development of business policy courses in US business schools, earlier this century. Widespread application came later, probably only during the last three or four decades. Strategy is derived from the Ancient Greek: *Strategia*, the art of a Commander in Chief, of projecting and directing the larger military movements of a campaign. Hitherto, it had been found in connection with military leadership and certain external affairs of sovereign states. Indeed, the extension of the word to the business world most likely followed from the very close similarity which could be drawn between running a business and numerous aspects of military experience. Organisational structure, styles of leadership and tactics have been so profoundly influenced by the much longer military tradition that it has been their most important example.

Perhaps most important have been the effects on tactics: concentrate your forces and your attention; aim where the enemy is weakest; change the battlefield when he is strongly entrenched; reinforce success rapidly; approach by the indirect route; achieve surprise whenever possible—all are military lessons which find a ready application in commercial strategy. It can be necessary to hunt around and choose examples from different ages, and some are inappropriate, thus, if mobility and swift response are considered, a Roman siege compares unfavourably with Genghis Khan's horses or German tanks. But the field of military history is so vast that for all tactics in business there is probably an instructive parallel to be found somewhere.

And how much more effective than business military examples can be to illustrate a commercial situation! Events pass quickly, reaction follows action, alternatives at points of decision are well defined and apparent to observers, relative force strengths are known, or at least in retrospect, and eventually, a decisive conclusion is reached. Of course, there are campaigns, such as the US adventure in Vietnam, which do not quite fit the pattern, but they are easily forgotten. Besides, there can be reason to select evidence where the intention is to learn from favourable example and success.

However, when there is much of value to be learned from a source, the unstated implication creeps in that *everything* from it is correct. Furthermore, military actions are nearly all so accessible, with battles of prime interest to historians since the start of recorded history, that the example is dangerously easy to over-play. For, though there are valuable similarities, there are also many, many differences between business and military organisations.

THE MILITARY EXAMPLE AND ORGANISATIONAL STRUCTURE

A formal army has upwards of 15 ranks, a number which have either been modelled on the structure of other armies, or have been bequeathed by a long history. Even in peacetime, before the development of the railways, 15 might have been too many, but the structure had to be suitable for rapid expansion in time of war. Once on a battle-field, the coordination and control of a very large body of men, either by sound, line of sight, or through dispatch riders, justified an elaborate structure of ranks for the dissemination of orders and collection of information, even though the functions carried out by the troops were simple. Introduction of railways and telephones led to the development of very much larger armies which retained the earlier structures. During the nineteenth century as firms expanded beyond a size at which the direct control of a proprietor was possible, in nearly all cases they adopted a form based on armies, the largest organisations seen up to that time. There was a disciplined hierarchy with rules, responsibilities, customs and periodic advancement all carefully laid out. Larger examples also created some staff positions adjacent to the central pyramid, after the military model. Early management writers, such as F. W. Taylor (1911) in the United States and H. Fayol (1916) in France, had direct experience of these bureaucracies and put over a conception of management and commercial life which was structured, ordered and mechanistic, so helping to reinforce the military message.

In practice, some of the shortcomings of rigid, bureaucratic structures in business applications had emerged early on. Such structures can accommodate size, but diverse activities are poorly served and diversity typically follows size. Around the time of the First World War some of the largest US corporations, such as Du Pont and General Motors, started to adopt a divisionalised structure as outlined by Sloan (1963). These could cover different markets, management styles, degrees of innovation and rates of growth and change between the various divisions. The new structures followed strategy, as they were adopted in response to actual needs and were ultimately affected by the intentions and direction of senior management.

Remarkably, it was to be more than four decades before this was pointed out and a wider appreciation of structural suitability for differing situations established. Several researchers—notably Burns and Stalker (1961) and Woodward (1965) in the United Kingdom and Chandler (1962) and Lawrence and Lorsch (1967) in the United States—had investigated actual situations. Among their conclusions was that while there is no single structure that is "right", a strict, mechanistic formal organisation with simple and efficient lines of control is preferable in organisations where there is little or no change and tasks are repetitive. By contrast, something more flexible and informal is needed where the emphasis is on change, adaptation and innovation. Furthermore, the structural need is most likely to be driven by market forces.

11

Though inspired by real conditions, the acceptance of these ideas has been slow and even now they are unlikely to have run their course. Various reasons may be cited: the inaccessibility of the texts; the very small sample of companies seen, in two cases; the conflicting message, at times, of the earlier "scientific-management" school; and some of the confusing and obscure terminology used. Thus—"mechanistic" or "tight", "organic" or "loose", "integration" and "differentiation", all with stronger associations to other disciplines, may be found. In the last few years, however, these research findings have been reported by much more popular and readable works.

Management theory and practice may have helped to modify the earlier bureaucratic structures, but arguably greater effects have followed the development of the electronic computer. In Shell's experience, manual methods required a certain small size of department, with a manager over it, in order to allow information flows to, from and between departments. Come the computer and the communication problem was eased so that information could now be accessed readily. Small departments and much middle management were consequently no longer needed. The whole structure looked lower and flatter.

While structure has generally adapted away from the military model, part of the reason may be because the military itself has not moved with the times. Today's trooper does a far more complicated job than his historic counterpart, so that the creation of an old-style citizen army in time of war would be a very doubtful proposition. Communications are incomparably better than in the past and still improving. Yesterday's army was organised to face a similarly formal structure on the battlefield, yet now the enemy is of a variety of formal and informal types. These differences alone would in civilian life lead to an organisation with fewer tiers.

LEADERSHIP IN BUSINESS AND MILITARY SITUATIONS

Some leadership requirements follow from the organisational structure. As commercial and military patterns have diverged, so too the appropriate style of leader has changed. Clearly a rather different person is likely to emerge at the top of a rigid bureaucracy with a tall, narrow structure than at the top of a broadly-based one with an innovative and relaxed style. However, there are other differences—some of which have always applied.

Armies are brought together for a specific purpose and a limited duration, which may be quite short. Information gathering is highly important, but it can be defined easily, typically by just two questions: "What is the enemy's strength?" and "What is his or her intention?" There is also an emphasis on leadership for brief periods of intense stress, with rapid decision-taking from a relatively narrow range of tactical choices.

The business leader, on the other hand, works in a less disciplined and less deterministic environment. Goals are more difficult to isolate and define. It is harder to generate a sense of purpose. The time-scale is indefinite and information requirements are far more complicated to address. Strategy really does have to be thought through in a business, whereas for the military it is ultimately determined in the political domain.

Concentration and diversification

Military theory and practice may have its most important application to business strategy in the principle of concentration. Concentrate your information flow on appropriate fields of enquiry; concentrate attention on things which matter; isolate what an organisation is good at and concentrate on it. The lesson has been learned so well that often concentration may be implied without the term being used—for example, with a phrase such as, "Critical Success Factor", it is unnecessary to add that it should be a centre of attention. Indeed, the principle pervades business strategy theory so thoroughly that its converse, diversification and dispersal, is overlooked. The impression can very easily be gained that concentration should always apply, but this is not so.

Although it sometimes appears as an axiom of military tactics, concentration is really just a principle whose emphasis should vary according to context and circumstance and used appropriately with care. Most theory on the topic dates from before the introduction of mechanised warfare, when concentration was needed to bring pressure to bear on the enemy at a time when the firepower of weapons was limited and both communications and mobility were poor. Today, when facing nuclear weapons, the appropriate tactic is unlikely to be concentration at all, but rather dispersal and rapid movement. Moreover, like part of the reason for military structure, concentration theory assumes that a formal army faces something similar. Pose a dissimilar threat, such as a guerilla force, and it need not apply.

In the business world, where there has been little or no attention to strategy and there is indecision over the future, concentration is likely to be quite the best advice for an interim period, because financial and management resources are almost certain to be dispersed, and there may be peripheral activities contributing little to the group. But move beyond an interim period and circumstances change, with an important distinction arising from differing time horizons: long or indefinite for business, much shorter for the military organisation. The relatively brief phase for the military ahead of victory or defeat leads to less concern for innovation and change than might otherwise be the case; concentration in this context may be a convergent process, deflecting attention from the active evaluation of alternatives.

On the other hand, whereas military capacity is determined largely by the public purse and political vote, a business is created through growth and innovation—two major, distinguishing features of its longer-term interaction with the market-place. Organic growth involves many processes which identify or consider fresh opportunities. These can develop a core, but typically will lead also to other activities, mostly related to the core but on occasion quite separate from it. Thus diversification is likely to follow growth and an overriding concern for concentration in the longer term would inhibit the size to which the firm could grow.

Risk and uncertainty are other factors which might modify the emphasis placed on concentration, as they are countered in different ways in the business and military settings. In both, they may be reduced substantially by greater research, intelligence and analytical efforts. Military risk, however, is finally overcome by achieving outright victory and establishing hegemony. Concentration on success thus tends to eliminate risk. By contrast, there is nearly always residual risk in a commercial situation, which cannot be removed and so must be accepted and managed. One course available is to adopt the tactic of the professional fund manager—to diversify. So the business may face risk and choose diversification, while the army's very different reaction is a redoubled effort with concentration. That is a big difference.

SOME CORPORATE ILLUSTRATIONS OF STRATEGIC DIVERSIFICATION

Unitech

Although Unitech has operated in only one sector since its foundation in 1962, its history has many instances of formal and informal diversification. The company started in industrial electronics, due to the market's attractions and to the fact that the professional background of Peter Curry, one of the two founders and the current Chairman, was in that sector. Subsequent success helped to endorse the choice and keep Unitech operating within its traditional activities.

The business developed as something akin to a venture-capital house, with market opportunities being isolated and then backed. The timing of some of the acquisitions has been influenced by their availability, but the intention to expand both organically and by acquisition was there from the outset. Evidence of a considered approach comes from the way that financial preparations are usually made well in advance. Marketing knowledge of the sector has always been highly important. Market forces to which Unitech has been responsive, and which have partly driven it, include customer developments, customer requirements and changes among component suppliers. Further examples of reactive policies come from success and disappointment with operations which cannot necessarily be anticipated. Successes tend to be reinforced with further investment, while disappointments may result in cut-backs, mergers or divestments.

A strategic review in the late 1960s examined the businesses in which Unitech had become established. The review noted that the company was a supplier to manufacturers, and this market niche was formally endorsed as a suitable place to stay. Principally in component marketing and the manufacture of power supplies at this time, diversifications into component manufacture and industrial controls were made a few years later. Though guided by certain broad target rates of return, both capital project appraisal and the capital needs of an activity have closely influenced the final choices of the businesses in which Unitech involves itself.

Diversification of sales, by customer and geographical area, has been another highly important influence on Unitech's development. In the late 1960s, turnover was entirely in the United Kingdom as this was where the company had started, but the United Kingdom then formed only 5 per cent of the total world market (the United States had the largest market, followed by Europe and Japan), and so a decision was taken to expand overseas. The obvious country in which to become established was the United States, but, with just a small UK base at the time, it seemed inappropriate to try to compete in such a large area straight away. Thus Unitech went into Europe first; by 1979 it was generating about 35 per cent of its sales there. The next decade saw a series of acquisitions in the United States, so that by 1988 the turnover split was around 50 per cent United Kingdom, 35 per cent Europe and 15 per cent United States.

Unitech's structure is of great interest as it has adapted to allow the growth of the business. Right from the start it has had a small group in the centre controlling investments in subsidiaries. Even in 1988, with a total group payroll of about 3250, head office personnel amount to just 18 in all, of whom 13 are executives. As the company developed, a range of functions that were once centred on the Chairman, have been progressively delegated, so leading to great changes to the Chairman's full-time executive duties in an increasingly large organisation. The basis for today's structure of four divisions was in place by 1977, similar activities being grouped into divisions and divisional Directors—each covering around five subsidiaries.

Financial structure has largely followed from the needs and preferences of the capital market. Starting as a private company, Unitech changed in 1971 to an industrial group with a public quote. This was partly to complete the financing of what was to Unitech at that time, a very large acquisition. Subsequently, acquisitions have usually been made for cash, raised mostly in advance through rights issues. These help to confine support to a group of investors who know the company's style and record. Throughout, the group's capabilities and financial resources have evidently been matched very carefully to the opportunities presented and the growth which has been achieved.

Success at Unitech has been associated with much diversification, from several causes. Some of it has followed directly from strategy, while other aspects have been essentially reactive, but with strategy as a conditioning influence. Other rapidly growing businesses may well find parallels with this experience.

De Beers

De Beers is certainly an example of strategic concentration, yet its survival for a century, with a majority share of diamond marketing for over three quarters of that time, has required more than just concentrating on current activities. There has been no time when this alone would have prevented the company's eventual demise; a straight projection from the current position would have led eventually to failure, with the steady exhaustion of production reserves and with changing circumstances for the marketing organisation. Constantly, therefore, De Beers has had to respond to fresh opportunities, market changes and a changing world. This has required adjustment and adaptation of the long-term view, indeed, it is difficult to find any major instance in the company's record, of the interests of the present compromising those of the future.

Although survival has required that De Beers' operations be open to change, the extent of its diversification is seen only in the wider context of the Anglo American group. De Beers' main holdings in 1988 were: Anglo American 38 per cent, Minorco 21 per cent and Anglo American Industrial Corporation 27 per cent. Anglo American Corporation was founded by Sir Ernest Oppenheimer in 1917, and it may be viewed as very much a diversification within a career whose mainstream was the diamond business. He had started as a diamond sorter in London in the 1890s, before moving to Kimberley as an agent for his firm. The closure of the diamond mines, during World War I, led him into gold-mining finance and, later, the formation of Anglo American. After the war, the purchase of German diamond claims in South West Africa, substantially with Anglo American paper, enabled Consolidated Diamond Mines (CDM) to be formed. CDM was to be instrumental in Oppenheimer's gaining power in De Beers, of which he was Chairman from 1929 to 1957.

Meanwhile Anglo American had become a member of the New Syndicate, formed from an organisation started by Sir Ernest in 1925. This first rivalled the Old Syndicate, in the wholesaling of rough diamonds, but, on its demise later in the year, the New Syndicate purchased its diamond stock. Further support for the diamond business came the following decade, when the size of the Anglo American group will have assisted De Beers in raising finance to build a diamond stockpile. When the diamond market recovered and the stockpile fell, after World War II, the cash flow from this stockpile was largely invested outside the diamond industry. During the 1930s and 1940s Anglo American diversified into base metals, coal and more gold, nearly all of it in Southern Africa. Industrial interests and substantial international investments followed from the 1950s onwards. Finally, the group was to assist De Beers once again during the diamond recession of the early 1980s, the worst for half a century.

All of this historic material might be slightly academic had not the De Beers' Chairman, in 1988, reaffirmed the principle that henceforth its investments outside the diamond industry were to grow in step with the diamond business. Here is an outstanding example of strategic diversification strengthening the original core activity.

British Aerospace

At British Aerospace it is possible to see both concentration and diversification emerging strongly from strategy. Soon after the company was privatised in 1981 there was a great deal of discussion about the future, culminating in a major strategy reappraisal in 1982. Its findings are reviewed every year and adjusted as necessary, but essentially it has set the course for development ever since. At the time, the company was strong in military aircraft and missiles and these positions of strength were to continue. More customers had to be sought for aircraft, missiles were seen as a growth area and a new fighter programme had to be established. Concentration was exemplified by several acquisitions of companies producing complementary products for the military market, notably computer software, munitions and construction. However, one of the fundamental views behind the 1982 rethink was a likely decline in the relative importance of future government spending. This made imperative a greater emphasis on civil programmes.

The group was already involved in civil aircraft, which was the first area where a much greater effort was made. Markets for civil aircraft were expected to expand and from this forecast the strategic implication followed. Space and communications had to be built up as another area of strength. A pilot school was started, partly in response to a perceived market need, and an enterprise group, BA Enterprises, was founded. Finally, The Rover Group was acquired, so diversifying products, markets and production.

Diversification is driven partly by the innovative process. Although the business units concentrate on their own projects they also produce a variety of new ideas. The innovation is really theirs, but a decision is needed on whether or not to back the new possibility—and this involves strategy. There are varying degrees of participation in a concept. Sometimes, as with unducted fans, a view might be taken that returns are some way off: in effect, the organisation sits on the sidelines, watching developments for minimal expense. When something looks promising, there are several phases of commitment possibly involving public funds, possibly not, before a project is brought to a stage at which it is a marketable proposition. Decisions then have to be taken on production and marketing. *Hawk 200, Merlin, Laserfire* and *Alarm* are all examples of projects developed at least initially with private money.

Progress and innovation have accelerated with the organisation's new commercial awareness. So many small ancillary businesses were being generated that a research centre was created to look at the development of technology and decide what was of use. Some ideas have been of direct application to operating units; others have been either sold, spun-off or put into BA Enterprises, which was created specifically for this purpose.

Dynamic innovation and change, concentration and diversification—all are demonstrated by many developments at British Aerospace which can, without exception, be related in large measure to strategy decided several years ago. Once the company has set a broad strategy, subsequent policy reacts to changing circumstances. It is difficult to see how much of the achievement could have been accomplished without a balance between, firstly, concentration and diversification and, secondly, between proactive and reactive policies.

3
Strategy and planning

While illustrating some of the divergence between historic military thinking and modern business strategy, the examples in the preceding chapter also help to show that planning and strategy are not the same thing. Much strategy occurs outside planning systems and some organisations with a formal strategy do not plan. Even where elaborate planning takes place, it is possible for it to perform only a minor strategic function. Strategy at the top of an organisation is part of leadership, and this may be expressed through planning. In very small businesses, leadership, strategy, authority and direction are all vested in one person, the proprietor. But in larger organisations these functions usually need to be delegated, to varying degrees. So the style of planning and the direction of strategy partly depend on the pattern of leadership and delegation.

STRATEGIC DELEGATION—SOME EXAMPLES

At British Aerospace there is substantial delegation of strategic issues. Overall strategy is formulated by a group at the centre which includes the Chief Executive and the Finance Director. Separate from it is the

Business Investment Committee, currently composed of nine Executive Directors who are Chairmen of the subordinate businesses. This committee oversees capital project appraisal and looks at the various ideas and proposals coming either up from the business units, or sideways from the corporate plan. The latter is participative and a monthly planning meeting is attended by the Chief Executive, with a major exercise carried out every Spring. Here consensus views are apparent in some of the targets used, notably, that costs are to be driven down by a third by 1992, assuming a certain sterling/dollar exchange rate. Delegation is also seen in matters such as the huge interface with governments around the world. This is widely dispersed and much of it has strategic consequences.

Corporate structure greatly affects delegation of strategic functions at Shell. Head-office activities are split, with most commercial matters handled in London, most technical issues in The Hague, and certain functions, such as personnel, being divided between the two. The basic operating unit is the country, with operational matters cutting across it. Essentially, all local duties are delegated to each country's Chief Executive Officer, who thereafter is largely autonomous. However, Head Office can intervene when two national interests become involved.

Unitech's pattern of strategic authority has developed markedly with the growth of the company and it is still evolving. The position of the Head Office, relative to its subsidiaries, is that of a catalyst, something similar to a friendly merchant bank. Responsibility for strategic matters and leadership is delegated through the four Divisional Directors to the Managing Directors of the subsidiaries. Expertise is held at the centre for perhaps three key areas and their related strategic authorities: human resources, financial matters and issues of group strategy. Head Office purposely has a low profile within the group and allows considerable autonomy. Emerging policies from subsidiaries may be overruled, but this is highly unusual, points of difference normally being resolved at an early stage.

STYLES OF PLANNING

These brief examples show that there is no single answer to how much strategic responsibility should be delegated or to whom. This matter influences the role of planning, and it has to be adapted to each situation. Still more complication arises from the differing activities the term "planning" has been used to describe. Here, four types may be distinguished:

- central economic planning
- planning to exercise power in a corporation
- scenario planning
- corporate planning with variable participation

Central economic planning

Central economic planning has been largely discredited, but it has implications for deterministic techniques and the role of forecasts. Central planning was a technique for running a large part of a national economy, or at least of the public sector, through a series of planning targets. The coordinating influence was expected to lead to greater efficiency, which could be promoted further by nationalising major industries and running them as government monopolies. The results of central economic planning were arguably inconclusive under the first post-war Labour Administration, with recovery and some continuing direct economic controls from wartime confusing any implications. However, the principle was decisively rejected in the light of the 1965–67 National Plan and of experience elsewhere, in countries such as India and Ghana.

Before World War II, it was recognised that methods for running very large commercial units needed to be improved to justify aggregating the major companies in a sector. Mathematical problem-solving techniques, together with much wider use of centralised budgeting, achieved many notable successes in coordinating the Allies' resources during the war. Significantly, these achievements were against a back-

ground of extensive direct controls, which greatly reduced the range of commercial risk. Physical losses were insured against, and markets were virtually certain, so supplies and operations were left as the only imponderables.

It was a different story in peacetime, and the early promise of a quantitative, deterministic approach was never quite fulfilled. In conditions of uncertainty there were applications in terms of the detailed running of a corporation, but not for steering the total strategy. For years it seemed that greater systems complexity and the prospective capacity of tomorrow's computers would finally turn the corner for determinism. However, it is now realised that suitable applications of such an approach are found only where the variables are few and mostly controlled, or forecast accurately.

Planning to exercise power and control in an organisation

A planning style whose prime purpose is to exert authority in an organisation has only a minor connection with strategy. It consists of a series of budgets to coordinate activities and establish targets for departments; these might be set after discussion, but not necessarily. Participative planning was developed partly to overcome criticism of such procedures by supplementing them with other functions. Planning today can channel power and authority, but normally aims to do much more.

Scenario planning

This technique is used principally to assess the outcome of differing assumptions on a future situation. An attempt is made to demonstrate a consistent set of features of, and implications on, some aspect of a corporation's affairs in the future. Coverage of the scenario may range wider than the corporate situation or be confined to a detail of it. Particular emphasis is likely to be placed on items which cannot be quantified, or those requiring a subjective evaluation and interpretation. The aim is to provide as full an answer as possible to questions of the nature "What would be the implications for us if . . . ?". Scenario planning was not widely used until the late 1970s, although Shell introduced it in 1971.

Corporate planning with variable participation

Participative planning is normally called "corporate planning" and is frequently known as "strategic planning". It involves taking a view of a corporation's future, conducting a thorough audit of its organisation, environment and markets, and then formulating a way forward. The exercise is drawn together in a final plan whose detail and budgets start to put a strategy into effect. However, just how much and which parts of a strategy are handled by the plan may remain an open question.

Planning of this nature became widely used in the 1960s, greatly stimulated by management writers such as Peter Drucker and Igor Ansoff. Drucker outlined a variety of principles and advocated rigorous analytical audits; together with strategic concepts, these would have led to planning. Ansoff addressed the matter more directly, and combined strategy with detailed participative planning—indeed the term, "strategic planning" may be attributed to his 1965 book *Corporate Strategy*. The ready acceptance of these ideas, however, owes much to other developments in corporate affairs.

The first of these was the inadequacy of economic theory to explain either what happens in a major business or how to run it. Resources have to be allocated, capital has to be rationed, information is needed and decisions have to be taken, and for all of these, something more than economic theory is required. As a partial solution, budgeting systems had expanded during the post-war period, sometimes being elaborated into long-term budgeting. Inevitably this led to demands for more information, better forecasts and an overall view to coordinate the several expanding disciplines requiring forward thinking. Consequently, from the late 1950s onwards, corporate planning was developed in several progressive corporations on both sides of the Atlantic.

But by 1970 corporate planning was being criticised. A system developed by a few organisations was inappropriate for the corporate world at large, and a more flexible, adaptable procedure was needed. Moreover some of the earlier benefits were elusive, notably synergy, and it was suggested that planning was in the wrong hands when carried out by the original budgeters. However, the systems and methods which corporate planning replaced were probably just as bureaucratic and ineffective, so at least little or no damage was done at this time.

The economic downturns in 1969/70, and, with much greater severity those in 1974/75, tested the arrangements for strategy and planning and found them to be wanting. Between World War II and the early 1970s, economic growth rates had fluctuated but had not actually declined, so cursory forecasting procedures had been sufficient. If the growth rate is steady, it does not matter if figures and information are several months late. Now, greater accuracy and a faster response were needed. Planning in general had to be handled much more thoroughly and professionally if it was to be valid.

Most of the articles on planning published at this time implicitly accepted the concept and worked towards improvements, such as refinements of procedures and, especially, of the forecasts. However, a few were openly critical, pointing out that whatever strategy and strategic thinking were, most if not all of these were happening outside the corporate plan. Such comments were found in books and articles mostly written by academics and read by other academics, and it is doubtful if they secured a large audience. Thus as late as 1982 it was possible for Peters and Waterman, in their best selling *In Search of Excellence*, to put across as an iconoclastic message "don't plan!". It seems that few took this advice literally, but in many firms a review and appraisal of just what planning was contributing was long overdue.

THE ROLE OF PLANNING

Justifying a planning function in a large organisation has not been difficult. Even those without planning departments and an actual plan perform many of the functions in other ways. The coordination of activities, the collection and dissemination of information and the execution of many strategic aims are all covered by the budgeting process. But expand this activity and those shortcomings appear which encouraged the development of corporate planning in the first place. Hence there is an underpinning of utilitarian functions which nearly always need to be performed, whether or not they are associated with the planning process.

Part of the case for planning is that although these functions can be carried out independently, a system, however simple, ensures the greatest benefit. Items can be overlooked, strategic reviews ignored and other points forgotten, without the sense of focus and intention a planning system can provide. Planning is not inevitable, though, as there are other systems which can take its place.

Many organisations use a structure possibly in conjunction with planning, with staff groups clustered around the Chief Executive. These groups make submissions, relay directives and prepare for the next submission. Napoleon is said to have run the French Army and much of France along these lines, and how much smaller are the problems of the present day company? The difficulty with staff groups on their own is that it is easy to overload the top person—or, rather, it is hard to find those who can accept such a level of responsibility. If an organisation has, say, 1000 employees, a low, flat structure, no planning and minimal bureaucracy, what happens? Whether by design or default, much becomes centred on the Chief Executive—possibly too much for his or her capabilities.

COVERAGE AND STYLES OF PARTICIPATIVE PLANNING

So planning is partly a response to organisational conditions and there is a basis of functions which justify the exercise, provided they are not carried out inefficiently. The scope, the broad limits to activities, and hence the time and resources which are likely to be needed are partly decided by organisational size and complexity. But, more important still, they are a consequence of the role of that planning in relation to the organisational culture. What really distinguishes different planning systems is whether they are imposed from the top (i.e. "top down") or generated predominantly by a participative process ("bottom up").

A "top down" planning process carries out the implications of a set of orders and supplies information relating to them. It is, in effect, a planning process for the exercise of power. Though nominally open to participation, little is likely to occur without the motivational influence of a record of practical effect. Top down planning is thus poorly suited to focusing on proposals originating far down the structure, so acting to the detriment of innovation.

By contrast, participatory or "bottom up" planning can be the prime avenue for individual expression. However, it is more complicated to organise, normally much more time consuming and prone to offer misleading views on the state of parts of a business: weak departments talk themselves up while strong departments are too busy to give the exercise much attention.

There can be an indistinct state in which "top down" and "bottom up" influences balance each other, but this is rare. Planning systems tend to fall into one category or the other, and the difference profoundly affects the efficiency with which they achieve whatever they are supposed to be doing.

THE STRATEGY-THROUGH-PLANNING ISSUE

Success for a planning system is partly a matter of it delivering what it is expected to provide. Everyone in an organisation could be happy with a plan which is unsuccessful, due to an ill-conceived set of goals and poor direction. More common however, is planning which is successful and valuable, yet the subject of widespread dissatisfaction through failing to achieve what were unrealistically set objectives. The production of a strategy is the outstanding example of such misplaced hopes. A strategy is widely expected to arise largely of its own accord from a planning cycle. In other words, strategy-through-planning is expected to occur.

The mechanism for this process is along the following lines. At the outset there will be no strategy, a lack of information and many uncertainties. The planning process gets to work, accumulates information and reduces uncertainties. Various goals emerge on a consensus of opinion, and an impression is gained of what the organisation has to do to secure competitive advantage—that is, to achieve and maintain increased profitability. Decisions will be needed here, but further analysis and planning rigour gradually narrow these down until eventually, the choices on these decisions are so obvious, so simple, that virtually anyone associated with the planning process could take them. They are then presented to the seat of power, which takes decisions as intended and so endorses a view arrived at through planning.

Strategy-through-planning relies on the partial replacement of strategic decision taking by planning. The latter may not actually take decisions, but it predicts what the solutions are almost certain to be. It needs at least four crucial assumptions for its operation:

- goals are clear-cut and self-evident
- competitive advantage is simple and easily isolated
- uncertainty can be dispelled, in part, by analysis and planning procedures
- the Board is willing to devolve a great deal of its power and handle what it retains in consensus style

None of these assumptions are completely far-fetched; even the last, while highly unusual, is by no means unknown—for example, something similar is seen in a situation where most day-to-day authority is in the hands of a group of senior general managers. A very large Board, with many non-executive Directors, an externally appointed Chairman and a collective style, is then faced by relatively few policy choices.

So strategy-through-planning is possible, but the assumptions needed for its operation make it a highly unusual special case in the commercial world. However, a partial contribution to strategy is feasible from the collective process, leaving much independent strategic authority outside the planning system. This is the typical situation in practice, and planning should not be dismissed just because it fails to deliver a complete strategy, or indeed, much strategic product at all.

SUMMARISING THE ROLE OF PLANNING

There is great variety in planning, and many of the hopes and aims for what it will achieve have been misplaced. With success partly dependent on a plan delivering what it is expected to provide, an assessment is needed of its current role. One approach here is to see what is being contributed to the planning process from each level of the organisation—what ideas and information are contained in the plan and where are they coming from. Then it is necessary to find what is coming out of the plan, who is affected by it, and in what ways. With the full picture, it is possible to decide whether or not the pattern is advantageous.

EXAMPLES OF PLANNING IN PRACTICE

Shell UK

Shell was among the earliest developers of corporate planning techniques, and the need to lengthen time horizons was a major influence behind the search for new methods. In the 1950s up to 1959, operating companies each made a one-year forecast of their activities. All of these were coordinated into a group budget, from which the finance department made a central cash-flow forecast. Horizons might have gone beyond the prospective year for the operating companies' own purposes, but for the group this was not strictly necessary.

In 1960, the horizon lengthened to three years as a result of a procedure known as Management Information Structure. This was replaced in 1965 by a seven-year horizon and a system known as Unified Planning Mechanism. Planning at this time involved a relatively simple process of projecting a single line of events. From 1971, the group found it necessary to think much further ahead on strategic issues, typically around fifteen years at Head Office. It is possible to detect the planning mechanism driving the approach taken to strategic thought, with an ultimate aim of providing a formal structure which requires managers to think ahead. Eventually, a situation is thereby created in which management's actions are guided by and related to the strategic needs of the business.

Also in 1971, the group introduced scenarios. At first these were treated as just a planning enquiry, with sensitivities on a few variables. Gradually this changed and scenarios played a valuable role in the introduction of forward strategic management attitudes. Events were soon to justify them fully, for the scenarios were able to show that certain current exponential growth projections were rubbish. Furthermore, they enabled the company to adjust rapidly to the new situation after the 1973–74 oil price rise and associated economic events. Today, two or three long-range scenarios are used to try to show what the picture will look like in 10–15 years; their implications can take some time—say a year and a half—to be appreciated. There is also a shorter range scenario with the principal purpose of testing the corporate planning assumptions. A new scenario package is introduced every two years and this can set a reaction in train.

Planning is reviewed formally every Spring, but what actually happens is rather more flexible. People talk across functions, relaying news to the centre early on, and so major changes never come as a surprise. However, getting some of the options to surface can be a problem, and part of the function of the communication channels is to highlight appropriately information generated away from the centre.

British Aerospace

At British Aerospace, there are currently around 100 major projects, many of them having time-spans which are very long indeed—in several cases it is necessary to be looking 25 years ahead. Thus all the main participants in the strategic process have to look ahead this far. Actual strategic management of the projects, within these very long time-frames which are the norm for the company, typically involves a careful mix of financial and engineering skills. Too many accountants and the project will not work; too many engineers and it will not pay.

Against that background the role of planning is essentially a secondary one which is still evolving. Planning is participative, and looks ahead for five years in detail, with a view on the following five—a horizon which is well short of many of the company's ideas. Planning is thus addressed to a limited range of issues and is not the only avenue of communication, nor the only system for obtaining and analysing information of strategic value. British Aerospace is large enough to support more than one system for many of the functions of planning, and its strategic demands are so great that it needs them.

Unitech

Unitech demonstrates very strong support from the centre for the concept of planning, coupled with a diversified, participative approach. Planning was first attempted about 15 years ago and subsequently the procedures, techniques and issues covered have all evolved in the light of experience. It is undertaken by the operating companies and is almost entirely for their benefit. The planning style used has to be seen to be necessary for their purposes. Each subsidiary produces a detailed plan for the prospective year and a formal outline for the next four years. These have two broad objectives: to revise continually the database for strategic thought, forecasts, the environment and so on, and, secondly, to attempt to set goals. Within these objectives, detail on matters such as competitive advantage will be addressed.

The main planning review from Head Office is carried out by the four Divisional Directors. On the final day there is a review of each division from the Chairman, including an hour's presentation on each company. The emphasis by this stage is very much on compensating for the topics the operating companies are less good at, such as the three areas of expertise held at the centre. While with crucial areas of marketing information, there never seems to be quite enough detail. In the end, the plans are primarily for the operating companies' benefit and it is as if someone just happened to have remembered to send the Chairman a copy.

4
Four ways of deciding tactics

Strategic contributions from planning are mostly tactical and a plan's ability to generate tactics can be greatly increased by the use of certain techniques. These may be broadly classified into four groups, but with considerable overlap between them. Planning does not depend on them and they can be used in isolation but, typically, the two are very closely associated. They should not be seen as general principles of universal application. However, at times, they can produce a set of tactics and just possibly a strategy too.

1 FINDING WHAT AN ORGANISATION IS GOOD AT AND CONCENTRATING ON IT

In this group, an approach to corporate appraisal is suggested to find what really makes an organisation work. The strategist is then usually assisted with some strategic guidelines. Terms used for the key points of an organisation vary, for example, distinctive competences, success factors, critical success factors and strategic excellence positions, and there are some important differences between them. A business may

33

be distinctively competent at something which is not a success factor. The latter need not be critical. A critical factor could be some detail such as credit control, but this is hardly the stuff of which a strategic excellence position is made. Nevertheless, it will be clear that many corporate qualities can be described by all of these terms. Besides, there is great value in pitching questions in several ways where the difference is between being efficient and being effective.

Evidently, too, this group of techniques is likely to involve an emphasis on concentration, as opposed to diversification. Having identified some items on which attention should be concentrated, within the information base, the strategic guidelines normally draw heavily on the military example. More concentration is likely to follow, but is not quite inevitable. The oldest of these techniques—strengths, weaknesses, opportunities and threats routine from the 1920s—leaves scope in its opportunities for innovation and diversification. But this is compromised by the prior concentration on strengths.

An objection to this group of techniques is that it does not automatically provide any tactics and still less a strategy. Nor does it even give a view on the fundamental basis of competitive advantage. Rather, it is based on the assumption that, with the right guidance, the strategist will produce additional insights. Ultimately, therefore, there is reliance on the flair of the strategist to identify points of corporate ability and to formulate a policy towards them. Here, at least, the planning system can give a lot of help. And, as with planning, the exercise might seem more worthwhile if it is not expected to yield a comprehensive strategy, but instead some tactics.

2 LEARNING FROM SUCCESS OR EXCELLENCE

This involves researching successful corporations to look for the causes of success and how success can be achieved. Such an approach is taken by a score of books from both sides of the Atlantic, most of them very popular, on topics such as business success and entrepreneurs, as well as on specific companies. These books are readable and tend to be strong on factors which are not open (or easily so) to numerical analysis. Generally, they give some very valuable results. However, a few criticisms may be made if any of the books are used alone. For instance, the standard of investigation is mixed and subjects are almost all historically successful, whereas the standpoint of some of the works requires examination of companies about to be successful.

A more formal method involving a similar process is given by the system known as Profit Improvement of Marketing Strategy (PIMS) which was originally developed by General Electric (GE) in the United States. This analyses many features across a database, which now extends to several thousand US companies. Variables include some non-numerical items and are evidently coded, weighted and then analysed to give the factors which have had the greatest influence on profitability. PIMS seems to be used mostly by companies to review subsidiaries, divisions and potential acquisitions.

3 STAKEHOLDER ANALYSIS

An organisation's stakeholders are any group or individual who can affect, or are affected by, the achievement of the firm's objectives. Clearly, there are many of them: customers, competitors, suppliers, backers, of several types, directors, employees, governments, government institutions and more. As progress towards strategic goals may be defined almost entirely by interaction with such groups, a strategy may emerge from analysing them—or, at least, so goes the argument in their favour. True, there will be some gaps, notably the production function, technical change and quality, but these are unlikely to be overlooked as they are so obvious.

This method is very strong on human issues, which are all but ignored by some other analytical styles. It also covers minor interests which, though of little importance at present, may be valuable in the longer term. There can be stakeholders, too, who are critical if the company is to achieve success, yet are difficult to relate precisely to current operations and awkward to analyse, unless addressed separately. The outstanding criticism of this technique is that customers are frequently of dominant importance, and there are ways of considering them fully without having to go through a formal stakeholder analysis. De Beers is one of the few examples of an organisation where this is not the case, as governments are the company's chief stakeholder.

4 INTEGRATED STRATEGY THEORIES

Integrated strategy theories provide a method for corporate analysis and a view of what will constitute competitive advantage; strategic recommendations subsequently greatly narrow the choices on tactical decisions. When used in association with a planning system, Integrated Strategy Theories may help to bring the prospect of strategy-through-planning distinctly closer, and in certain situations could even set a strategy. Not surprisingly, they are widely used, but they are subject to severe limitations, and success can depend on stringent assumptions. Two of these approaches will be examined.

Strategic portfolio planning

Portfolio planning is perhaps best associated with the Boston Consulting Group (BCG) and that group's original matrix. Other, more complicated, matrices have appeared, but as their utility depends largely on their underlying assumptions and on the care taken in their application, complexity is a matter of little concern.

The outline of the BCG matrix is simple. Draw two axes and place growth rate on one and market share on the other. Divide the area into four squares and label three of them: "Star", "Cash Cow", and "Dog", and the fourth can have any one of several names, such as "Wild Cat", "Problem Child" or, most commonly, "Question Mark". No prizes for getting the right names on squares. The organisation is then divided into "strategic business units" which are plotted on the matrix and managed; those with promise being encouraged, the no-hopers being divested, cash generators being balanced against those needing investment, and so on.

This matrix has been so widely criticised as to have been virtually lampooned, on the grounds that it overlooks too much and that many of its direct prescriptions can lead to mismanagement. The matrix, after all, might even have helped to inspire, through its implied quest for market share, some of those acquisitions down the years which later went wrong. Furthermore, the assumptions needed for its operation really are far-reaching. The experience curve must apply to production or, in other words, there are economies of scale. Related to this in part is the fact that product life-cycles must be seen in markets. There is consequently reduced uncertainty, a basis for some valuable forecasts and, most importantly, some of the competitive advantage will be cost-based. With such a background, it may be questioned as to whether a matrix is needed at all to recommend a strategy of growth and low costs.

However, it is when the matrix is used as an analytical tool that its worth appears—indeed, it may even be argued that its pitfalls are all so obvious that anyone with any sense will not fall into them. When applied to a particular situation, it is necessary that the matrix is calibrated, markets and market shares assessed, strategic business units isolated and the crossover between growth and decline in an industry decided. All are simple concepts which can be, however, very hard to put into practice. In the end, the product portfolio will have been so positioned relative to its markets as to bring the successful management of monopolistic competition much closer. Quite a task for a planning system and one which will take it significantly further towards strategy-through-planning.

The Harvard school of strategists

The Harvard Business School has a long tradition of basing strategic thought on rigorous analysis. The strengths, weaknesses, opportunities and threats (or SWOT) routine from the 1920s has been mentioned (see page 34), as too has the 1950s concept of distinctive competence which the leader had to seek out and concentrate on. More recently, an Integrated Strategy Theory has emerged, best known through the writings of Professor Michael Porter.

Following the Harvard tradition, Porter's approach is firmly grounded in the appraisal of the organisation and its markets. For companies, the value chain is used, a technique which involves examining all the linkages through the entire production process and analysing how they generate costs. Although this was a fresh insight for Harvard, parallels may be drawn between this and the Austrian school of economists' ideas on the production function, with their emphasis on the detail of its structure, whether the linkages are few and simple, or many, complicated and capital intensive.

In Porter's approach competitive advantage is seen as stemming from a firm's sectoral structure, within which it must be positioned favourably. Sectoral profitability is determined by five competitive forces:

- pressures between competitors
- pressures from customers
- pressures from suppliers
- the threat of new entrants
- the threat from substitutes and technical change

Weakness from just one of these forces can gravely impair an industry's margins. With the five forces as a base, competitive advantage is achieved through just three courses:

- low costs
- product differentiation
- securing a market niche

In this process, the role of the strategist is crucial to provide appropriate guidance and steer the organisation forward, relative to the pressures around it.

Here another parallel can be drawn with the Austrian school, for this view of the strategist is something akin to the Viennese conception of the entrepreneur as a motive force, a catalyst for change in the business cycle. Mostly, in economic theory, conclusions and decisions are supposed to follow by logic from the coincidence of functions. In practice, however, the hardest thing in business life can be to take a decision, pick up a telephone and actually do something about it. So Porter really puts the strategist in the picture—and a highly appealing picture it is, with a powerful and deservedly popular message.

But the model has its limitations, too. These centre chiefly on the view it takes of competitive advantage. Clearly, there is more to industry profitability than the sector's five competitive forces. One method used by later writers to fill the gaps is to decorate the model with the stakeholder interests which the basic version omits. This answers one criticism, but introduces the problem that competitive advantage is rather more complicated than the simple model suggested by Porter. Besides, there are other fundamental shortcomings to which the stakeholder approach is unsuited.

Though conceptually different to the BCG matrix, the five forces model is similar, the competitive advantage resting ultimately on the cost structure of the firm and the successful creation and management of monopolistic competition. Yet these are only a part of the possible origin of monopoly power. Significant omissions are non-price barriers to sectoral entry and the producer surplus, or economic rent, arising from major assets, which are difficult or costly to duplicate. Of course, these exist in most organisations in varying degree, while some property and natural resource companies are dominated by them. Somehow Porter's model appears to overlook them. Where they are very small, they might be justifiably ignored on the grounds that they will express themselves through the cost structure. But there are so many organisations for which this is simply not valid, for example, Shell and De Beers.

In Porter's scenario the essential condition of an able strategist is of outstanding value, and the point might have been given greater prominence. As it is, little is said about the individual, yet a successful strategy requires first finding someone of ability.

THE CONTEXT OF US STRATEGY THEORY: A POSSIBLE SOURCE OF DIFFICULTY

Despite some of the criticisms which may be levelled at US strategy theory, its achievements in terms of clarifying many issues have nevertheless been considerable. Besides, it has been by far the greatest influence on strategic thinking in recent decades. Virtually every aspect of it must apply somewhere, as supporting examples can always be found. However, as it is unusual to find a work on strategy using a sample of more than ten companies, the context of many apparently complete and convincing treatments really needs to be defined. Though they may be valid for a certain style of situation, this may have a different character compared with some of the corporate norms elsewhere.

The organisational contexts of the United States have more similarities than differences with those of other countries, but some of those differences are important. Furthermore, nearly all US writing on strategy has come either from management consultants, or from academics-cum-consultants. Though it is never stated, it often appears that behind their words is really a case study of a US mainstream consultancy client. Clearly, if this organisation is not quite typical of the United States as a whole, and the United States itself is not the same as the country in question, there should be concern for the context of the analysis.

THE US MAINSTREAM CONSULTANCY CLIENT

US opinions on what life is really like in the United Kingdom tend to be a source of mild amusement to the British, so it is with a comparable risk that a profile of a US mainstream consultancy client is attempted. It is a relatively large company, not necessarily in the top 50 but probably within the top 1000 of US corporations. It is diversified, with much managerial activity decentralised to its operating units or divisions, whose relationship with head office is remote. Activities are largely, if not entirely, in manufacturing typically engineering, and with the company's technical function being the dominant discipline, accounting comes a poor third to law in the managerial pecking order. Headquarters may be in an eastern state, but operations and the corporate culture are centred on mid-west cities with a small town style where change is slow, venture capital is still largely unknown and Wall Street is a world apart. Local prejudices against big banks in big cities, which helped to frame much nineteenth century banking legislation, linger on. The view of the outside world is changing, but it still scarcely affects corporate policy, and exports, though rising, are below 10 per cent of turnover. With accounting and information seen as lowly functions, the management accounts and information provision have poor coverage and much uninspired detail—their presentation may be unclear and they are often late. However, on a brighter note, the productivity of both capital and labour, though increasing only slowly, still compare favourably with returns in Europe and Japan. Moreover, some aspects of quality, too, are strong.

Whether or not the mid-west is affronted by such a caricature, it fits US management writing well; particularly so for the Integrated Strategy Theories. Immediately, the theorists improve information provision. Where systems and accounts are poor, an alternative method, such as the value chain, really comes into its own. Competitive advantage follows a comparatively simple pattern, while non-price entry barriers and asset returns are small enough to be ignored. Management thinking is greatly enlivened by contact with outsiders. There are major strengths on which to build and a long overdue review of activities produces a list of potential divestments and widespread adjustments to market positions. Tactics for the medium-term become clearer and things start to happen. Somehow it all fits, it all works, but it is in the United States, not some other country.

In the United Kingdom in the right context, all of the four groups of approaches to strategy formulation may be used either alone or in combination for their tactical implications. It is rare that nothing from any one group applies, or at least gives some insight to tactics. Equally though, they may not necessarily provide a comprehensive solution on their own and expecting them to can be dangerous.

41

5
Competitive advantage

There will be organisations for which competitive advantage is itself a strategic goal. Generating and sustaining a superior level of profitability will clearly be a high priority for most of them, but there are a few exceptions. It is possible, for instance, to have tactics which lead to a decline in margins for an interim period. Some goals, too, may not necessarily be reached by the steady reinforcement of success. There are also, of course, non-commercial organisations where modified criteria are needed. Nevertheless in commercial life, ultimate success most often requires the achievement of competitive advantage for as long a period as possible. So it certainly is important and, as previously discussed, its nature affects the strategic process and the broad limits to what can be expected from a planning system. If the outline of competitive advantage is simple, strategic prescriptions may also be simple and more of them may arise from planning.

Here it must be re-emphasised that simplicity concerns just the *outline* of competitive advantage. The Harvard school view, for instance, starts off by being simple but gets complicated when detail is introduced. In its view, competitive advantage stems from a firm's cost structure, the appropriate management of the forces of monopolistic competition, and the expertise of the strategist who positions the firm relative to these forces. The strategic choices are then between low costs, product differentiation, or finding a market niche. The idea of cost reduction may produce an image of an accountant with a hatchet and a short term outlook, but in such a case the scope for profit improvement would soon be exhausted. Further progress requires:

- relating the firm's production function to the overall picture of supply in the sector
- establishing whether or not there are geographical limits to declining costs
- assessing if it is possible to compete on price

If, in terms of the last of these, it is not possible to compete on price alone, market acceptance will require better product quality, in the broadest sense of that term, to establish demand and hence the sales volume which will lead to lower unit costs. Thus the route to a strategy of low costs may not be entirely clear at first, and clarifying it will take much time and trouble. Similarly, exhaustive effort can be required to define, first, just what constitutes product differentiation in a given situation and, then, how it may be met. If that is not complicated enough, consider the corporation with tens of markets and hundreds of products.

However, in outline, the modern Harvard school of thought suggests that competitive advantage is simple, and this limits its application. Nevertheless, it covers much ground very well, and, if other documented sources of competitive advantage are aggregated with it, a body of theory is built up which may explain nearly all situations. So to the Harvard school's model must be added some further sources of monopoly power, such as assets and non-price barriers to sectoral entry, as well as the introduction of certain stakeholders. Moreover, as a general rule, human factors and the strategist, or entrepreneur, in particular are often inadequately served and are sometimes ignored. Human resources need a much higher profile from strategy.

WINDOWS OF OPPORTUNITY

Competitive advantage is further complicated by some of the cross-products which can arise between its causes. An example is the successful management of transient opportunity—that is, of windows of opportunity which may not necessarily occur but frequently do. Once capability and capacity in an industry have been established, a variety of deals arise. These may concern operational matters, marketing issues, financial markets, the purchase and sale of companies and so on. It is as though a window of opportunity opens for an indeterminate, but probably brief, period and a rapid decision has to be made if the conclusion is to be profitable. Naturally, most of these decisions will be centred on those with authority for strategy. The resulting competitive advantage may be seen as a product of:

- the organisation's capabilities and capacities
- the flair for profit of whoever handles the incoming deal
- the passage of time, which raises the chance of opportunities occuring

COMPETITIVE ADVANTAGE AND SECRECY

Another influence which may affect and condition strategy and competitive advantage is secrecy. When an organisation, such as a bank, is strong and perceived to be so, something in human nature perceives it as even stronger when information is concealed and a certain mystique built up; if everything about it is known, it is assessed only for what it is. This illusion of strength may be turned into competitive advantage. Besides, secrecy itself complicates life for competitors and introduces uncertainty into their tactical moves. Secrecy may also be an essential adjunct for surprise.

Secrecy varies greatly from sector to sector and depends chiefly on the nature of the business, its structure, staff and culture. For example, disclosure rules in banks and unincorporated businesses provide a legal basis for it. Physical protection, restrictive covenants on employment and the use of information may raise valuable secrecy thresholds. However, in the corporate scene at large, informal rules and culture are the most powerful barriers, and in a variety of almost indeterminate ways add to a firm's competitive advantage.

DE BEERS: A STUDY IN COMPETITIVE ADVANTAGE

While there will be situations with a simple competitive advantage, others, evidently, are complicated, some highly so. The potential complexity may be illustrated by considering the history of De Beers Consolidated Mines during the past century. Several of the features which have contributed to its strength have varied greatly in importance down the years, and today may have a minor influence. Nevertheless, these features are still highly relevant to attempt to explain how a dominant market position in the diamond sector was first established and then maintained for so many decades. In no particular order of merit, 10 of these features have been as follows.

1 Leaders with vision

Leaders with vision have been essential to De Beers and may well have been crucial to its competitive advantage. Indeed, its only period without such a leader—the quarter-century from 1902—was one of decline, with control of diamond production and marketing being lost. The subsequent initiatives to re-establish such control came principally from two outsiders: Solly Joel, who purchased a new competitor, the Premier Mine, in 1908 and sold it to De Beers in 1917; and Ernest Oppenheimer, who gained control of South West African production before coming to power in De Beers.

The company's founder, and first chairman for the 14 years until his death in 1902, was Cecil Rhodes—a man of undoubted vision in his other empire-building activities. His direction was essential to consolidate a fragmented industry. He started with a small business offering a steam-powered pumping service to the owners of diamond mining claims around Kimberley and, principally, to those working the pipe on a farm purchased from two brothers named De Beer. Grade varied widely with location and depth, and so during bad times, payment was sometimes accepted in the form of shares in the claims. In this way, Rhodes gradually emerged as the largest claimholder at a time when it was becoming imperative, for technical reasons, to merge the workings.

However, the diamond market was cyclical and Rhodes foresaw that, ultimately, control of production and marketing would be needed if conditions were to be stabilised. The various steps towards this position were spread over several years. First, control of the De Beers mine was secured. Then, acting in collusion with Barney Barnato, the largest operator in the nearby Kimberley mine, Rhodes acquired its second largest interest, the French Mine. Next, he sold diamonds heavily, forcing the price down and under these conditions was able to pressure Barnato to merge with him to form De Beers Consolidated Mines. Three smaller pipes in the Kimberley area were then bought and, with a production monopoly, Rhodes worked to secure legislation to control smuggling. Lastly, he contracted to sell De Beers' entire output to a London syndicate of ten broking firms, later known as "The Syndicate", and referred to here as "The Old Syndicate". This was in 1893, 21 years after Rhodes had first arrived in Kimberley.

De Beers' next outstanding leader was Sir Ernest Oppenheimer, Chairman from 1929 to 1957, and arguably the most powerful man in the diamond industry from 1926. There are numerous details from his career which demonstrate vision and a primary concern for the long term outcome. Two may be illustrated from the period of his Chairmanship: the establishment of the Central Selling Organisation between 1925 and 1934, and the stockpiling of diamonds during the 1930s. The Central Selling Organisation was intended to be durable and has indeed proved to be so. The diamond stockpile, which is believed to have reached a peak in 1937, probably included sufficient gem quality goods to have supplied well over five years' demand at the levels ruling in the late 1920s. It is difficult to see how either of these achievements could have been made without the company's leader looking to market conditions a generation ahead.

Entrepreneurship and forward-thinking have been demonstrated also by Harry F. Oppenheimer, Chairman from 1957 to 1984. One outstanding example was the advertising campaign for diamonds which he personally instigated in 1938. This is remarkable as one of the very few campaigns in which the final product is advertised not by its immediate producer, in this case the diamond cutters, but by an organisation further up the production chain. Significantly, perhaps, the campaign has been about market creation, as opposed to raising market share. Aiming to increase overall market demand for a product, with the returns filtering through intermediate production stages, requires that a longer view be taken than would otherwise be the case.

As Chairman, Harry Oppenheimer was chiefly responsible for a variety of agreements with other producers and interested parties. There have been several temporary defections from the Central Selling Organisation and some re-negotiations here and there, but quite the most impressive feature of these agreements has been their stability. Deals were intended to last for many years in a changing world and, for the most part, it would appear that they have done so.

2 Leaders with political involvement

Another and quite distinct leadership quality at De Beers has been the political involvement of some of its personalities. Cecil Rhodes was a member of the Cape Parliament from 1881 and became Prime Minister in 1890. Sir Ernest Oppenheimer was Councillor for Kimberley in 1908, Mayor in 1912 and a member of the South African Parliament from 1924 to 1938. Harry Oppenheimer is perhaps best known politically for being the principal backer of the Progressive Party, but before this he was, from 1948, a member of the South African Parliament for five years.

Political involvement probably made its greatest contributions to De Beers' competitive advantage during the 1890s, when rampant smuggling of diamonds was curbed. There was much effect, too, in the 1920s, when legislation was introduced which seems to have had three aims: to control output of diamonds by South African mines, to curb the power of the Old Syndicate in London by establishing a Union Diamond Board, and to help the small diamond mining operators to the detriment of large companies. However, in attempting to help small operators, the Diamond Control Act of 1925 omitted alluvial sources and, after two large, new discoveries during the next two years, which eventually were bought up by De Beers, further legislation would have been needed to re-establish production control. The full development of a Diamond Board outside Sir Ernest's control might have posed the greater threat. However, possible government criticisms were answered by the establishment of the New Syndicate in 1925, followed by the demise of the Old Syndicate and, in 1930, the creation of the Diamond Corporation. Significantly, this was within three months of Sir Ernest becoming Chairman of De Beers. The Diamond Corporation included the producers in the Syndicate on an equal footing with the distributors, so ending years of mistrust and discontent. Official production control seems to have been forgotten at that time, but, in any case, it was soon to be applied in the 1930s, for commercial reasons.

3 Handling the stakeholders in a manner consistent with a long-term view

De Beers is one of the few examples of a company for whom customers are not the dominant stakeholder. Indeed, it may be questioned just who the customers really are—the diamond brokers, the cutters, the retail jewellers or the final consumers? All are vital to the industry and important within the demand pattern. Taken together, though, they are less important to De Beers competitive advantage than are the suppliers of rough diamonds. In most cases this means that the chief stakeholders are the governments of the host countries. These are: South Africa, Namibia, Botswana, Angola, Zaire, Tanzania, Ghana, Guinea, Sierra Leone, Brazil, Venezuela, Australia, The Soviet Union and several minor producers.

Though they are not major producers, the United Kingdom, Belgium, Israel, India, the United States and Japan may be added to the stakeholder list, being the countries in which De Beers principally operates and sells. To all governments it is necessary to establish that working with the company is a better option than either attempting to market output independently, or having a cutting industry of a different size, or whatever that particular government's interest happens to be. Near-term aims have to be balanced against the long-term interests of the industry as a whole, dissatisfactions have to be weighed against returns, and so on. It is a complicated picture and a difficult one to maintain. Many Foreign Offices would be pleased to be able to placate all of De Beers' stakeholders at the same time.

4 Control of diamond production

De Beers is often thought of as a diamond production monopoly, and it was virtually that when it was incorporated in 1888, having perhaps 90 per cent of world output at a time when few diamonds were produced outside South Africa. Control was soon extended through curbs on smuggling, and dominance was enjoyed for a decade. However, a severe decline followed the discovery of the Premier Mine in 1902 and then later, in 1908, the alluvial fields in German South West Africa. By 1914, De Beers' share of Southern African ouput was down to about a third by weight and probably slightly less by value.

World War I led to the acquisition of Premier and, in its aftermath, Ernest Oppenheimer formed Consolidated Diamond Mines to purchase German diamond claims in South West Africa. But by the time these interests were merged with De Beers, discoveries of diamonds in several West and Central African countries had ensured that the world production share of 30 years earlier would never be regained.

From this time more producers, and the widely differing proportions of industrial and gem-quality stones from the mines, complicated the pattern. However, it was probably not until around 1960, with the rise of Soviet production, that De Beers' share of capacity, by value, fell below half. Today, the group controls directly about a quarter of world mine production, by weight, and probably slightly more by value. In addition it produces most of the synthetic industrial goods, although these are very much less valuable.

Aside from the financial returns, control of a proportion of production played a crucial role in the initial creation of a unified industry. Later, too, it was essential in enabling Sir Ernest Oppenheimer to reunify South African production and establish the New Syndicate. Today it may be questioned whether the Central Selling Organisation could be run in quite the same way without at least some production control within the group, for its working depends partly on being seen to be strong and that strength would be reduced were it not for the evident backing of substantial mine capacity.

5 Control of diamond distribution

The control of diamond distribution contributes greatly to De Beers' competitive advantage. The market for industrial stones and polished gems fluctuates, yet a high degree of price stability is introduced through market control, as well as enabling the needs of the final market to be balanced more closely by mine production outside the group. Furthermore, the market is managed in such a way as to accept the range of stones produced. That is, to take all the awkward shapes, grades and colours as well as the fine, easily polished gems.

The market is conducted through a system of 10 diamond "sights" a year, for which the requirements of clients are submitted. Boxes of diamonds are then put together to reflect the clients' needs, the background of demand from other sources, final market conditions and the profile of the grades being produced and stocked. Market regulation is thus exercised through:

- the numbers invited to sights
- the quantities of stones in the sight boxes
- the composition of grades
- the price
- the orchestration of production changes
- stockpile fluctuations

Although large differences may be seen on any of these points, over time, the long-term interest of an orderly market leaves the group with only limited flexibility in the near-term. For example, prices at sights have in exceptional circumstances been subject to a temporary surcharge, but at all other times have moved upwards by amounts which have been justified and sustained by market conditions. This leaves very little scope for discretionary, flexible pricing.

When the Diamond Corporation was formed in 1930, there were some external syndicate members, but these were bought out the following year under conditions of financial distress. The marketing company, the Central Selling Organisation, was formed in 1934 and, in 1946, a separate subsidiary for industrial stones was established. The group is believed to have always handled a majority of world output by value and today the proportion is as high as ever; the company officially putting its share at over 80 per cent. Informally, the proportion may be put slightly higher.

6 Financial strength and diversification

To maintain its control of diamond distribution in the long-term, De Beers has to be able to survive recessions such as were seen in 1970–1972 and, much more severely, between 1981–1984. During a recession production can be cut, mines can be encouraged to retain more stock, and those further down the production chain can help too, but, ultimately, De Beers must have the financial strength to stockpile current output. Clearly this is substantial as there is the balance sheet, close relations with the rest of the Anglo American group and some long-standing banking relationships, backed by a name and reputation for good business. Besides, there is the history of several decades of rising values for the main item of collateral—the rough diamond stockpile itself.

So strength is there undoubtedly, but how much is extremely hard to estimate. It must be partly evaluated in relation to need, and here, too, there is obscurity, since the cost of buying in and stockpiling say a year's output, is not directly available. Most of the numbers can be assembled and an inspired guess taken, an exhaustive exercise, but that is all.

De Beers' strategic diversification through portfolio investments has already been discussed as an important feature of its financial strength. Diversification may also be seen as a counter to the depletion of the group's mines. These are wasting assets and unlike some other businesses, re-investment in them does not ensure survival. Undoubtedly, diversification raises De Beers' competitive advantage.

7 South African corporate legislation

South Africa is not alone in tolerating corporations with large market shares—there are other countries where there is distinctly more active encouragement, such as Sweden, Italy and Japan. But there are some major countries in which De Beers could not operate in its current form, so this degree of toleration must be seen as a major part of the company's competitive advantage. Moreover, South African commercial policies have been quite remarkably consistent and stable down the years, notably towards mines. Favourable conditions are created for enterprise, there is legislation for much technical disclosure, and capital investment is treated favourably. However, the resulting profits are taxed heavily through both a system of lease payments and the corporate tax structure.

There are also certain details of South African corporate legislation which can apply to all companies but which particularly benefit those with a complicated structure. Regulations restricting the disclosure of financial information and those permitting cross-shareholdings are examples.

8 The size of the industry and its strategic importance

One reason advanced for the success of central marketing in the diamond industry is its size; large enough to be a major business, yet not so large as to be of outstanding concern to possible competitors and national governments. It is neither so large nor important as, for example, the oil industry, with annual sales of rough diamonds totalling around US $4 billion in 1988.

Historically, diamonds were of strategic concern in the early 1940s. The United States needed large quantities of industrial stones and the London stockpile might just have fallen into enemy hands. Also, the exploration of the Soviet Arctic in the 1950s and the development of diamond mines there (at heavens knows what cost) may have had a defence motive. But such fears have receded since the development of synthetic production, which can be sited virtually anywhere. It now meets about 80 per cent of world demand and has greatly reduced the real cost to industrial users.

9 The nature of the product

Most commodities are homogeneous and easily traded, but diamonds are the exception. Each stone is different and has to be sorted, graded and valued before coming to the market. At this point it must be re-evaluated by someone with appropriate skills and experience. In other words diamonds are a highly differentiated product and their trading is confined to a few people whose abilities are not easily learned. Competitive advantage is conferred on the employers of such people.

10 Management and advertising

Numerous managerial functions contribute to the competitive advantage of De Beers. Rough diamonds have to be purchased around the world in a variety of formal and informal ways. The market has to be managed from site to site. Information has to be gathered and assessed, commercial interests have to be balanced, and so on. The loss of any of these functions could gravely impair profitability; most of them would be costly to replace as they require experience as well as skill, both of which are at a premium in a close-knit industry.

The advertising campaign also confers significant competitive advantage, as it raises demand in mature markets and penetrates others in which diamonds have been all but unknown. With expenditure running at an annual rate of $130 million, in 1987, the advertisers are brought together with representatives from producers, cutters and retailers in London every year to help capture the latest mood.

Complexity and effect of De Beers' competitive advantage— a conclusion

An insider could well add to these 10 points. As they stand though, they are sufficient to demonstrate that competitive advantage can be complicated and consist of many factors, few of which are open to numerical appraisal; even those that are may make a contribution whose relative strength is impossible to assess. Some of the factors handled in subjective terms can be crucial to the operation of the business, but it is difficult to describe them more precisely than to say that their role is substantial.

De Beers is a monopoly, yet its former Chairman Harry Oppenheimer, once claimed that there was no one associated with it who did not benefit from it. Such a view might sound hollow to a small diamond cutter wondering whether to accept or reject a sight box. But, within the broader context of the diamond industry over a period of time, it is another matter. All participants benefit eventually from price stability, ordered markets and central, organised promotion, since without these the final market for diamond jewellery would otherwise be much smaller. Price stability raises demand in mature markets such as the United States and Europe, by an indeterminate, but certainly significant, amount. Promotion plays a part too: without it, the new markets in the Far East would hardly have been touched. Taken together over time, the absence of these factors alone would halve the industry's present size and possibly make it much smaller still.

And what of the final consumer? The world market for diamond jewellery in 1988 is around US $30 billion (at the retail level). De Beers' gross profit on diamond account is about three per cent of this figure, of which a proportion is attributable to mining operations. Returns from wholesaling and marketing of over 80 per cent of the world's diamonds will thus be rather smaller. For this the consumer gets the assurance of price stability in an important piece of jewellery and the tradition of steadily rising values, at least in terms of US dollars.

Herein, perhaps, is the key point from De Beers' experience of creating substantial competitive advantage and maintaining it for decades. Voices of discontent there may always be—those refused invitations to

54

sights, small businessmen with the prospect of always having to work in the shadow of a large and powerful organisation, however benign— but, in the long run, everyone involved must feel they have benefited. Arranging such a state of affairs requires a patient approach to business, with a low profile bordering, at times, on total secrecy.

6
Forecasts and forecasting

Forecasting is central to the formulation of a strategy: indeed, its limits may closely condition what that strategy will be. It affects the time horizons used for goals and tactics, the scope which should be given to planning, and the decision as to whether or not planning should be undertaken at all. Some tactics are crucially dependent upon a background of forecasts—whether to lead in development, for example, or to follow others depends on the ability to forecast product life-cycles and reaction speeds. Organisational structures are affected too. With the degree of uncertainty low, possibly reduced by forecasts, simple rigid structures and much use of deterministic methods become possible. In other situations with much change, many forecasts and residual uncertainty, something more open and flexible is required. Once some forecasts have been made, even strategic prescriptions can follow from the technique of Portfolio Planning.

One reaction to the disappointments with strategy and planning in the last decade has been the attempt to improve forecasting; results were not as anticipated, but with better prediction they would be satisfactory. There has thus been a spate of papers to this day which, in effect, aim to show something can be forecast better. However, another conclusion drawn widely during the 1970s is that forecasts do not work, cannot be expected to work, and so are a pointless exercise.

COVERAGE AND DEFINITION

Most of the difference between these two positions hinges on the definition taken of a "forecast". Here a broad definition is used, since for most of the time, organisations have a view of the future even though they may not be aware of it. Thus forecasts may not go by that name, but appear instead as hopes, views, assumptions, projected data, and so on. They may have been considered in great detail, with an extensive background of information, or scarcely at all and without information. According to this broad definition, virtually every business proprietor forecasts; what differs is how good he or she is at it. A few appear to be very good and tend to show a certain flair for the concepts handled, coupled with a thorough grounding of information.

OTHER REACTIONS TO UNCERTAINTY

Important though they are, it is possible to operate without forecasts. Essentially they represent just one of several methods to reduce uncertainty, or manage it, or both. Portfolio diversification is another example of these methods, but it tends to raise the internal complexity of a business and the managerial requirement. Planning is also used in part to reduce uncertainty and if there are few or no forecasts, the style chosen is likely to emphasise rapid adjustment and reaction to changing circumstances. None of these examples are mutually exclusive; all may be applied together—and typically are.

THE PAST FORETELLS THE FUTURE

Forecasting is a specialist function, nevertheless, several points may be made. Of these, the most important is that nearly all forecasts rely heavily, if not entirely, on the principle that history repeats itself, that the past may be used to foretell the future. This notion is used in a variety of ways. In some of the more complex applications involving mathematical models, it can be far from clear that this assumption still applies. Its most simple and widely used form, though, is to take a piece of information and make a projection from it. An apparent trend is thus assumed in some statistics, which is then advanced into the future.

Nor will such an approach be erroneous if indeed there is a trend and it is steady. And, as in the early days of corporate planning, it does not matter with these conditions that the exercise is performed after a long delay using historic data. A technique which attempts to place greater attention on the quality of such forecasts is Zero-Based Budgeting. This came into prominence when it was adopted by some US Government departments under the Carter Administration. By taking the budget bases to zero each year, an annual re-think is encouraged and the likelihood of simply taking last year's trend and extending it is reduced. Clearly, success depends partly on how much forecasting and information gathering is done. Attitudes may be rooted in the past, after all, even if the opening figures are not. But the approach can at least be a positive step.

Considerable elaboration of basic trend projection is possible: data may be smoothed statistically, trends fitted formally, non-linear functions isolated, and so on. And success need not necessarily depend on fate and fortune delivering a stable trend. Some of the most successful applications, using variants of the principle, rely critically on choosing the conditions under which a projection is made. Thus they will not necessarily offer a prediction at a given time, but at a time of their choice. In effect, such methods are criticising the underlying assumption that history repeats itself. Rather, history repeats itself only some of the time—a simple but valuable distinction.

Another development from trend projection is to look for patterns or cycles of events. These can take an almost infinite variety of forms. Some may have relationships of strict, predictable cause and effect, stipulating quantities and times, while others are just a sequence of general events. Some occur for reasons which are understood, yet others are observations of a train of occurrences whose causes and relationships may be partly unknown and possibly spurious. Time-scales can vary from a matter of decades downwards. So cycles are a

58

mixed bag and their quality often needs attention, but they can provide an analytical start. They might also just help to overcome that outstanding criticism of trend projection—its failure to isolate turning points.

The product life-cycle is an important example of a pattern of events whose usefulness rises the more one knows about it. It is valuable to know that there is such a cycle operating, even if its form and duration are unknown, but it is much more valuable if detail on its magnitude, direction and time-span are available.

REVIEWING HISTORICALLY BASED FORECASTS

The questions to review all forecasting activity from a historic base are similar. First, there is the information which has been used; this varies from gossip, opinion, reported experience and so on up to the harder quantitative categories such as prices and statistical time series. Information is not necessarily wrong just because it has come from a low-grade source, or right because it appears to be "hard". Some "hard" information is really just an interpretation of qualitative material.

A second issue is how the information has been handled—whether by formal, mathematical techniques, by less formal approaches such as graphs and charts, or by informal discussion. Then there is the issue of just who has been involved in the forecasting process—their level in the organisation, experience of running forecasts, responsibility and association with the outcome. Most important of all is to question the underlying assumption that history is expected to repeat itself. Why has there been a historic trend? Why has a pattern emerged? What are its fundamentals and what assumptions are needed for them to continue to hold?

A frequent omission from trend projection and its variants is the attempt to balance the time-scale of the historic situation with the span of the projection. There are no hard and fast rules here but, clearly, a two-year series is inadequate to back a ten-year projection. Similarly,

attaching equal importance to data from 20 years ago as to last year's figures, is likely to be inappropriate for a projection for the next six months.

FORECASTING APPROACHES WITHOUT A HISTORIC BASE

Arguably, there are no forecasts which are entirely free and independent of the past, but some are relatively so and make no use of historic data. One of these is to construct a notional model of events on which forecasts can be based. The break from the past is not quite complete, as the model itself is typically derived from economic theory, relying heavily on history and experience. In addition, the model is likely to be tested against actual situations and only accepted when it is producing successful results. The hidden assumption then applies that the future will resemble, in some way, the conditions of the dry run.

Forecasting methods that are used to predict the reactions of another party rely on the principle that theoretically infinite discretionary reactions are often limited in both number and scope. Isolation of these limits can lead to successful predictions when a confluence of events arises on which a decision will be needed. The decision taker is then subject to historic constraints, and so has a restricted choice, which may be anticipated. The break with the past is once again incomplete, but at least historic data are not used.

Another distinct forecasting approach is to judge the mood of the market, and the current of opinion and to project forward as opportunities arise. Any amount of historic information may have brought the entrepreneur to the point of decision, but suddenly, that is all history. A creative response becomes necessary to changing events, a response which has been triggered by the current situation in isolation from what has gone before.

Lastly, the managed outcome to a forecast can avoid historic influence, although here the forecast is akin to a goal. The organisation first sets a forecast and then proceeds to engineer events to achieve

6 FORECASTS AND FORECASTING

the desired outcome. This could be entirely a forward looking process, but in practice is unlikely to be. Forecasts, targets, goals, objectives, or whatever, are almost always set with reference to the past, while incoming market-related information ought to influence the tactics by which they are to be achieved. It is hard to shake off history completely.

USING FORECASTS

Criticism of forecasting is easy, to the extent that forecasts are almost never entirely correct. But the usefulness of a forecast depends on whether it can be made with a workable degree of accuracy. In many applications it is not strictly necessary to have an accurate, quantitative outcome. Rather, the direction of change in a variable and the likelihood of its continuation in that direction may be sufficient information. Quantities are valuable if they are there, but if of secondary importance, their absence may not invalidate the exercise. Similar remarks can be made, too, in situations where the isolation of a turning point dominates other issues.

Some forecasts are exposed to results so that success and variances will be registered externally. This applies particularly where a variable to be forecast is involved in a financial market, and money is either made or lost. Elsewhere, with imprecise feedback or none at all, a basis for successful results may often be judged from whether the other players in the market can be identified. After much attention to a forecast, it is as though the organisation has broken clear of the woods and the other competing forecasters can be seen on the open ground. These may be a journalist or two, consultants, people from the City, as well as opposites in other organisations. Many of them will actually be known by name to a forecaster with a thorough grounding in the variable's fundamentals. Once the forecaster is in that position, success, if it has not already been achieved, is then close at hand.

7
Where you want to go

All organisations need to set objectives, and many probably do. In a similar way to informal strategy formulation, almost every Chief Executive must have a general idea of his business' direction. The setting of objectives may never be discussed, or discussed only within an inner circle of executives. The objectives may never be written down, or may be confined to the minutes of a meeting, so that the ultimate aims of the organisation are unknown to most of its employees. But whether formalised or not, isolating objectives will be an essential part of the strategic process and the organisation's leadership.

Although objectives are likely to be modified over time, in the light of the information from a planning cycle, they are independent of the latter's time horizons and the limits of the associated forecasts. Objectives can apply from the present onwards, as a financial guide-line might, or they may be attainable only in the very long-term. They may refer to specific quantities and times, such as achieving a certain market share within three years, or be in general terms, for example, attempting to have a cost structure as low as or lower than anyone else's. Whatever their form, objectives should clarify the strategic direction.

MISSION STATEMENTS

Sometimes there is a mission statement, which adds to, qualifies or even replaces some of the objectives. It can go by another name, such as "corporate vision", and it may cover specific goals or merely some supportive aspect of the strategy. Its prime purpose is communication and so it must capture some vital feature, express it briefly and so concisely that it is remembered. Because of this limitation, the mission statement is unlikely to be a comprehensive statement of objectives and, typically, will omit a majority of them altogether.

The importance of distinguishing the mission statement from the vision which gives rise to it is especially acute in the larger organisations. At Shell, for example, a concise, overall mission statement has been attempted without clear success. Either the statements are just too general in a business of its size and complexity to fulfil their intended purpose, or else they are too specific for everyone to react to them. A cascade of statements for various levels and activities fails to achieve a unified sense of direction; while a statement for each of the three parts of the business (Shell UK Exploration and Production, Shell UK Oil and Shell Chemicals UK Limited) is perhaps the best possible compromise.

Such difficulties are unlikely to arise in the small or medium-sized business. In a smaller group it is much easier to produce a statement with which everyone identifies, with the communication channels adopted being really just a reflection of the style of leadership.

SETTING OBJECTIVES

In setting objectives, the leader's task will evidently be easier if he or she is leading everyone towards conditions which they all regard as desirable and attractive. There may be highly demanding steps along the way, involving distinct challenges, but these will be surmounted if the ultimate goals are feasible and consistent with aspects of the current situation known to all.

Almost inevitably, such a conception will require some change and probably also some growth. Furthermore, buoyant conditions are likely to be needed to formulate the vision. For, although setting objectives is partly intended to help carry the organisation through patches of difficult trading, during a temporary decline time horizons are drastically reduced. So much so, that it may be impossible to turn attention away from near-term cost reduction, a process quite at odds with the outlook needed to encourage strategic management. The whole strategic process receives a setback in a recession; it is much harder to step aside from the daily clutter of events at such times and envisage a more optimistic world.

With the onset of firm operational conditions, the strategic process may be encouraged. It is doubtful that objectives ever arise solely through the flair and inspiration of the leader. Flair may play the major part, but a background of information will be needed to formulate objectives and is essential for their review. Assembling information closely resembles the outline of a planning cycle and, in part, the resulting objectives may be considered to have arisen through planning. Naturally, there is great scope here for participative methods, particularly for those objectives which are in public domain.

The principal areas of investigation are likely to be defined by the headings which follow.

The corporate culture

Corporate culture may be defined in widely differing ways, but business philosophy and corporate values will be of prime concern. It is often misleading to consider these in isolation from the aspects of corporate life they influence, but nevertheless such values can lead to the formation of objectives. For example, there are:

● corporate values which restrict, limit or select operational activities
● ethical standards towards any stakeholder group
● customs and attitudes affecting quality, service and managerial time horizons
● historic common purposes and identification with them
● standards of security and secrecy

The stakeholders

Customers will head nearly everyone's list of stakeholders and they are considered under the next section on competitive advantage. Other stakeholders, however, will still be of critical importance, so justifying separate objectives:

- profile of the employees and their turnover
- investment in training and education
- composition of and policy towards the owners or backers of the business
- objectives towards other stakeholders such as government agencies and the local community

The sources of competitive advantage

This will probably be the largest topic, with the possibility of great detail on operations and market-related matters that are potentially suitable as objectives. A careful reappraisal is needed where any other objectives are inconsistent with aspects of competitive advantage. Such aspects include:

- organisational size in relation to current and prospective suppliers, competitors and customers
- final markets served
- geographical spread of markets
- market needs met by the business
- market stability
- profiles of suppliers, competitors and customers
- operational position relative to suppliers and final markets
- technologies used by and affecting the business
- nature and complexity of operations
- the speed of change: whether to lead it or to follow
- capacities and capabilities for organic growth and for acquisition

Financial objectives

Like other general objectives, financial performance measures carry a more powerful message when used in combination. Growth of earnings per share must be the most widely used financial target and normally gives the best indication of performance. However, there can be situations where growth of assets is what really matters, growth of sales being of prime importance for a limited period. Furthermore, earnings need to be qualified by the risk accepted to generate them and by their quality. Factors which have to be considered are therefore:

- growth of earnings per share
- growth of assets
- growth of sales
- gearing levels and earnings cover
- quality and stability of earnings sources

Organisational structure and style of management

Clearly, the structure must be consistent with the prospective implications of other objectives. The topic is particularly important in the small, growing businesses where hitherto there has been little choice over structure. Considerations include:

- delegation and centralisation of functions
- relative size and role of the group at the centre
- organisation by product, market, location, subsidiary, division, or none of these
- influence of leading personalities
- scope given to participative procedures
- number of organisational tiers

A profusion of objectives will probably arise from which a few of the best should be selected. They should be broadly based, with some applying far into the future and several suitable for widespread dissemination. Those which can be communicated widely must now be relayed as far down the organisation as possible to generate working targets. An elaborate corporate planning system is a great advantage here, as individual targets can apply to each centre of planning accountability. Almost certainly, two sets of targets will be required: one for next year and the other for the medium-term—around three to five years hence. Targets for the next year may show little or no change from what they would otherwise have been, but for those which lie further ahead, profound influence can be expected from strategy.

Formulating a mission statement

With a provisional set of objectives, the art of formulating a mission statement comes in summarising an aspect of them. There is a conflict between coverage and brevity. Capturing the essence of a strategy in a sentence is the ultimate ideal.

8
Where you are now

Once you have decided provisionally where the organisation ought to be, would like to be, or simply hopes to be, it is necessary to determine where it is at the moment. The resulting audit can be quite brief, but typically it is a lengthy process. It is difficult to see how all but the simplest of strategies can be formulated without, first, an impartial assessment of where the organisation is and what its resources are.

Audits used to be based largely on financial analysis and numerical information. These audits had the great advantage of being relatively brief and consistently applicable to any organisation, large or small, in any activity, provided accounts were produced. Today the dangers of such an approach are widely recognised: derivation of figures can be just as subjective as any other information; on their own, they provide only a minor part of the picture, with marketing issues in particular, tending to receive insufficient attention. Overcoming such objections had led to elaborate procedures and it was difficult to cover comprehensively all types and sizes of organisation without becoming very general. Here, many of the items may not apply to a given situation, and so it is a useful preliminary exercise to isolate those which do. The principal headings of an audit are given in the rest of this chapter.

The organisational structure

- whether organisation is by product, activity, market, or none of these
- geographical locations of principal operations
- number of organisational layers
- number and length of the lines of control
- degree of interaction between departments
- extent of change and innovation required and actually developed recently in operations and products

How the organisation is run and the role of planning

- how capital investment decisions are taken and by whom
- which activities report directly to the centre
- extent of the day-to-day participation by the central executive group in the organisation's running
- which activities are consciously delegated away from the centre
- whether planning exists and, if so, the form it takes
- who contributes to planning and at what level
- purposes of the final plan and who is affected
- whether the final plan is dominated by top-down directives

Growth or fundamental decline

- whether under performance is attributable to passing misfortune, poor management within a satisfactory sector, or the demise of the sector
- recent success which may mask a decline within a sector
- whether unsuccessful, declining activities are concealed by successful ones
- the sectoral life-cycle: when it arose and why, its historic growth pattern, and any outstanding causal factors
- technological development of products and processes
- conceptual view of technical change
- association with favourable technologies and rejection of unpromising ones

The corporate culture

- the business philosophy
- the personal values of the organisation's leader
- corporate values in relation to size and structure
- subjective differences between the organisation and its peers among competitors
- activities supported evidently from the top
- whether parts of the business are product driven or value driven
- cultural constraints introduced by current profile of personnel and the organisation's policies towards them

Overall quality

- product design, performance, finish
- service design and performance
- speed of delivery, breadth of distribution, customer service
- what the markets perceive as being quality at a particular price level
- attitudes affecting total quality

Human resources

- isolation of key personnel at all levels
- assessment of current capabilities and capacities
- facility and cost with which the size of the labour force can be varied
- managerial capacity and degree of current utilisation
- motivational influences other than money
- assessment of morale and motivation at different organisational levels
- institutional aspects of industrial relations
- historic pattern of training and the scale of the current effort in relation to sales, margins, employee and organisational needs

Assets

- assets at book value
- assessment of market value
- their capacities and degrees of utilisation
- estimation of actual returns on notional market values

Economic conditions

- economic variables affecting the organisation
- sensitivity to changes in the principal variables
- economic outlook over the near and medium-terms

Political environment

- extent and nature of the political interface between the organisation and its sector, both in its home country and overseas

Tax and legal framework

- assessment of the importance of any tax or corporate legislation to the business
- importance of activities in terms of generating tax revenue
- social acceptability of the organisation and its business

Products

- product range
- feedback of marketing information to design
- whether development is driven principally by market or technical issues
- whether product life-cycles apply
- competitive items
- new, mature, old or obsolescent items

- ease or difficulty and speed with which products can be copied
- market shares
- costs and margins

Pricing

- whether cost based or market related
- decision-taking structure and information for discretionary pricing

Markets and customers

- identification of customers and their characteristics
- functions performed for them by products
- factors influencing and triggering a "buy" decision
- aggregation of customers into markets
- open competition and niche markets
- geographical spread of markets
- market sizes and fundamentals—growth or contraction
- extent and nature of market diversification
- market information and ease with which it is obtained
- subjective assessment of the standing of the organisation's name and products in the market

Marketing, promotion and distribution

- marketing costs in relation to turnover and profit
- expenses at the margin in relation to market penetration
- broad comparison with competing efforts affecting market demand
- estimation of effectiveness, however subjective

Competitors

- identification of competitors
- direct, indirect, current and potential competitors

- product portfolios and degree of overlap
- market shares
- estimates of quality, costs, delivery, service, geographical positions, promotion and technology
- management capabilities and reaction speeds
- view on current strategic intentions
- summary of strengths and weaknesses relative to one's own organisation

Potential competitors

- attractions of the sector: currently visible margins made in it
- ease of entry to industry: information barriers, monetary barriers and non-monetary barriers
- potential acquirers of competitors
- strategic rationale for suppliers to move downstream and customers to move upstream

Suppliers

- proportion of supplier's output taken up by one's own organisation
- proportion of purchases made from each major supplier
- margins generated
- delivery
- reliability
- financial strength
- quality
- service
- credit terms

Operational functions and production costs

- principal features of the production process
- full costs and costs at major stages for a given volume
- overheads
- cost comparison with competitors at home and internationally

Systems and accounts

- detail, coverage and accuracy of management accounts
- speed and frequency of returns
- clarity and brevity of their presentation
- historic ratio analysis with major trends taken back at least three years

Finances

- strength of balance sheet
- cash flow fluctuations during year
- standing with banks
- number and variety of facilities
- likely financial resources under differing scenarios

Profile of uncertainty facing the organisation

- isolation of where forecasts are needed with the horizon over which they are to operate
- assessment of where forecasts may be attempted and the time span over which they may have workable accuracy
- responsibility for making forecasts, and at which organisational level forecasts should be made

9
Putting the strategy together

In the aftermath of the audit, a number of questions arise. Six of these will have widespread application.

1 SHOULD YOU AIM FOR GROWTH AT THE PRESENT TIME?

This question opens up a huge field of enquiry. It may be useful as a first step in distinguishing shorter-term factors from those with a longer time horizon, and issues which are external to the organisation from others which are within it. The near-term will be up to about three years and includes solving current problems in preparation for ultimate growth. Adverse economic circumstances may come about and it may be necessary to complete initial penetration of wider markets. Internally, various inadequacies with the company's products could rule against an immediate growth programme, while a whole range of shortages and bottlenecks, notably associated with skilled labour, could take time to remove. Such matters are predominantly managerial problems, but they can delay a strategy.

In the longer term, the fundamental decline of a business, or its sector, is the key argument against continuing without changing the objectives. However, in other situations caution is called for in spite of seemingly attractive commercial opportunities—for example, where these might lead to an overcommitment. Large contracts are a case in point, as their subsequent loss could jeopardise an organisation. Another example is where a sector moves towards maturity and suddenly the necessary scale of enterprise needed to survive rises by a factor of 10 or more. This happened in the oil and diamond mining industries in the nineteenth century and in the motor and aircraft industries earlier this century. Today, such a development can be seen in parts of the electronics sector. The survivors have to face massive growth and manage it, but among the other players will be those who choose to direct their efforts elsewhere.

For the most part, though, growth is accepted with enthusiasm. The future may be fraught with uncertainty, but the risks of standing still are even greater. Indeed, a strategy for limited growth, or none, is essentially a tactic which can be used over only a limited period. Ultimate objectives and the course towards them must be clarified, and any temporary difficulties overcome. All of these are possible, given time.

2 DO YOU HAVE THE RIGHT TECHNOLOGY?

There are two sides to the technology issue:

- avoiding a declining technology
- associating with an emerging field at the time when the returns for the necessary effort and investment are at their greatest

Together , these issues are probably the outstanding reasons why large corporations rise and fall. Technology is also among the hardest strategic issues to handle, since it is a topic for which the past is an unreliable guide to the future. Developments within a technical category may be associated with some trends, but potential competition from a different technology is quite another matter. Obsolescence can be gradual or sudden and it may be virtually impossible to predict events, let alone to put a time-scale on them.

Technological questions affect methods and processes as well as products. Analysis could start with the recent pattern, the rate of technical change and whether or not there have been discontinuities. Development speeds in relation to the level of research and development expenditure are a line of enquiry which may help to isolate a highly promising area. Thus early progress is often slow so that high, additional expenditure is consequently misplaced, but likewise, the end of a technical cycle normally sees developments becoming harder and increasingly costly to uncover. So the middle is therefore the place to be, but the cycle is stylised; technology follows very different patterns and time-frames.

Some products and processes are driven not so much by their associated technical change, as by their market acceptance. Technology may make a product possible, but whether it will be made, and when, can be almost entirely marketing issues.

3 IS PERFORMANCE IN THE SHORTER-TERM MORE IMPORTANT THAN IN THE LONGER-TERM?

The message from organisations successful over the longer-term is that ultimate interests should never be compromised for the shorter-term unless there is some really compelling reason. However, in the commercial world such reasons frequently seem to arise and taken on their immediate merits, they may not necessarily appear to damage the longer-term outcome. Thus windows of opportunity may come, pass quickly and never recur. Market situations may develop and if not exploited soon, will attract competitors. Acquisition targets need to move fast or risk losing their independence. A strong stock market orientation, for this, or for other reasons, may require an emphasis on certain near-term issues. There may be such a high level of financial and operational gearing that the repercussions of just one poor result outweigh the advantage of several years of better returns achieved with a long-term outlook. In all of these situations, success requires concern for the near-term and usually, too, a rapid response.

Such influences detract attention from the longer-term aspects of strategy so that acceptance of the wider implications of strategic matters becomes harder to establish. Certainly, there can be no option but to follow many near-term pressures, but a firmly held strategy to restore ordered progress should never be far away.

4 WILL THE CORPORATE CULTURE ALLOW YOU TO ACHIEVE YOUR OBJECTIVES?

The culture must be consistent with the prospective needs of the market, the composition of the workforce, the organisational structure, the organisation's activities and any other aim of strategy. Although corporate culture has been highlighted by earlier writers as a crucial factor determining an organisation's excellence, there are few evident examples in the United Kingdom where it has been consciously moulded to meet a strategy. One approach to changing it is to build on the culture which is already there, encouraging its development in the desired direction. This is almost inevitably a lengthy process, and an early start is essential.

Such a pace of events was quite out of the question at British Aerospace in one of the outstanding strategic cultural changes in recent years. Formerly working on government cost-plus contracts under public ownership, a radically different, commercially orientated culture was needed for the innovation and diversification into several civil programmes, which have been added to existing areas of strength. So market change led to the need for a rapid cultural adjustment, which was accomplished by combining it with organisational change. Layers of middle management were removed and their authority centralised for a time before being redistributed in a manner which would encourage the new commercial orientation and attitude. There is scope for confusion in such a situation unless there is a prior explanation of what is happening and why. People remember when power and authority are centralised, but their redistribution tends to be overlooked.

5 HOW MUCH INNOVATION DO YOU NEED?

Innovation and change are nearly always the product of a combination of factors; in particular the organisational structure, the capabilities of the workforce, the stimulus from the market and the strategic lead. A shortfall in terms of just one of these can impair the entire effort. Outstanding products of innovation may be identified, but its objective overall assessment is very difficult. Thus the best method may be to decide whether a greater emphasis on change is now required than the organisation has seen in recent years, considering products, processes, markets and competing developments.

6 ARE THE ORGANISATIONAL STRUCTURE AND STYLE OF OPERATION APPROPRIATE?

Structures are a consequence of the nature of operations, the needs of the market and of employees, the extent and pace of change and the potential for growth. The operational style may be bureaucratic or open, and the central executive group can have a distant or a close relationship to everyday matters. The board may contribute little executive ability or a lot and, while there is likely to be a participative planning system, this need not be so.

All of these issues affect and are affected by strategy. Furthermore, they are nearly always constrained by vested interests, so that, without intervention, structure and management style they are unlikely to develop to meet the needs of a fresh direction. Indeed, quite the contrary: experience frequently shows a build-up over time of bureaucratic tendencies, with associated rising overheads.

TACTICAL SUMMARY

There are several methods of summarising a corporate situation in order to produce tactics. To ensure that all important points are identified, a combination of three approaches is suggested here, each with a different analytical emphasis.

The first is a variation of the analysis of strengths, weaknesses, opportunities and threats. A strengths and weaknesses analysis may be too formal a treatment in many smaller businesses, while opportunities and threats will have been isolated by the preceding six questions discussed above. Consequently, the approach may be simplified to asking what an organisation is good at doing and what it is not so good at; that is, what it thinks it is good or bad at doing, how it appears to outsiders and how it compares with its main competitors. The list should be long with much of its content being of a housekeeping nature, as opposed to being of strategic significance. However, the line between the two levels is indistinct and, in any case, many mundane difficulties may be obstacles on the path to a strategy.

The second approach is to look for "critical success factors", or some similar description for what matters. Again, two tiers may be distinguished: major and crucial. A long list will be composed largely of items which are not strictly strategic issues, such as adequate security for the computer files, but whose absence could certainly delay or jeopardise a strategic programme.

Lastly, a detailed view of competitive advantage should be attempted. This is likely to depart significantly from the two preceding methods, since many minor sources may not be critical factors in themselves, or relate to anything an organisation seems to do particularly well, but may contribute in a cumulative manner. Analysis of causes and the maintenance of superior profit should be made as detailed as possible. These may include production related factors; market issues; quality; design; assets; the people at director, executive or other levels; stakeholders; windows of opportunity; and secrecy. The list should be treated as open-ended and include the principal and positive aspects of discretionary strategic choice.

Concentration

The analysis of strategy so far will have aggregated a large agenda of issues, opportunities, difficulties and shortcomings, all of which might have seemed to be of strategic relevance. Now, in relation to the other priorities, many are of sharply reduced significance. Almost all, when set against the background of the original objectives and the emerging strategy, may be interpreted as tactical matters. Some will be resolved quickly by the executive, while others may need redoubled attention in the months ahead. Gradually, a convergent process of concentration will narrow them down. If there are 25 items now, there may be 15 after the first year, 10 after the second year and perhaps 5 left after five years. The extent and tempo of the process will be set by the opening position, the view of the strategist and the vigour with which it is pursued.

Diversification

As already discussed, the principle of concentration is essential, and in the absence of any other strategic direction it is probably the best advice. However, the fundamental narrowing of options into the future should be balanced by a degree of diversification. An indication of the extent and timing of this will have come from the answers to the opening six questions. But now an outstanding skill of the strategist comes into play: balancing diversification against concentration in order to achieve the original strategic objectives.

Other tactics

Immediate tactics are determined largely by current capabilities, and choice widens only when these have been altered. A decision to compete as a market leader or a fast follower, for example, is determined by the portfolio of forecasts and reaction times. Isolation of product life-cycles thus largely decides whether fast following is even a viable proposition, or whether instead there should be a greater emphasis on innovation.

Likewise the nature of growth in the immediate future is largely conditioned by the past. If the growth is to be organic, there is a certain pace at which fresh products, customers and markets can be introduced, depending on how closely developments match historic experience and the managerial capacity. Acquisition is an alternative, but the rate of historic disappointment here is around one case in two. An acquisition strategy critically depends on the ability to handle and manage the acquired organisation and such a capability takes time to establish.

10
Reviewing the strategy

ARE CURRENT RESOURCES CONSISTENT WITH THE STRATEGY?

The process of review is never far from the surface of a strategic cycle. Once there is an outline of the objectives, tactics and the programme of things to be done, it must be compared with current resources. Of these, finance, the assets base, personnel and management capability deserve particular attention.

Finance tends to be either almost impossible to alter, or quite easy to change radically and quickly. There tends to be a cross-over point for an organisation's credibility, above which additional financing facilities are readily available. Below it, even the far wider range of financial institutions today, compared with a decade ago, can fail to meet the hopes of a firm in difficulty. Assets might be hard to add to at short notice, but over time, they are dependent chiefly on finance.

Human resources are quite another matter, however, with management abilities and capacity of particular interest to a strategy. For example, in Unitech's operations in the electronics sector there are plenty of opportunities around and no shortage of organisations prepared to finance them. What ultimately constrains the growth rate is a matter of personnel. Expanding a skilled and semi-skilled labour force is a costly and time-consuming activity.

Management capability—or rather the lack of it—is possibly the outstanding reason why new strategies fail. It is not the strategies' content; on the contrary, they are likely to contain many things which should have been done years ago. But if all these excellent ideas and proposals are put in at once, management becomes over-stretched. It might then have been better if such a substantial programme had not been attempted in the first place.

Appraisal of both capacity and the demands of strategy will be subjective. A useful start can be made by distinguishing direct developments of the current situation from aspects of the new order which are departures from current practice and largely unknown. These latter are likely to involve far more time, trouble and expense.

REVIEWING WITH ALTERNATIVE SCENARIOS

At various stages, the strategic exercise may be greatly helped by introducing alternative scenarios. What happens to all the qualitative factors if assumptions about market demand, competitive reaction, operations, etc., are altered? Try to create a worst case and a best case. Under what conditions or outcomes would the objectives of the strategy be reviewed, revised or abandoned? What has to happen for the resources considered adequate for the most-likely-case scenario to become insufficient? In this event, would further resources be raised, or the subsequent strategic sequence be postponed? Attempts to answer questions of this nature might just disclose an outstanding flaw in the organisation's intentions, and certainly prepare the organisation for those unexpected events which will inevitably arise.

REVIEWING THE ROLE OF THE CORPORATE PLAN

Some aspects of strategy are unlikely to be handled by a corporate plan under any circumstances, but can still leave a substantial role for planning. And now planning can be expected to perform a valuable function in putting a strategy into effect. Accordingly, its utilitarian purposes should be reviewed. Just what is it supposed to be doing? Budgeting? Information gathering? Coordinating? Communicating? Getting people to think? Any other purpose? And who are the contributors to it and what levels are they at? What are they contributing? Similarly, who gets something out of the plan and at what levels? A few simple questions of this nature may confirm a positive role and help to prevent the spread of bureaucratic tendencies for which planning has been criticised.

By the time a prospective year's plan is to be undertaken, it is likely to be too late to influence the strategic direction of events through planning; instead, this should be attempted with the view two years out and further. Planning's strategic function is then to see how proposed developments look from the various organisational levels and how strategic guidelines might be modified for future plans. Irrespective of whether guidelines have been imposed from the top, or generated participatively, their significance and their value in the interpretation of strategy must be evaluated.

SENSITIVITY ANALYSIS

Sensitivity analysis really comes into its own once the budgets have been produced, as the figures involved allow the use of computerised methods. Particularly useful where high variances are inevitable within a few months, the limitations of sensitivity analysis are easy to forget once the numbers are entered. For instance, numerical quality varies widely, projections beyond a year should be treated with extreme scepticism, and it is virtually certain that there will be inadequate allowance for qualitative features.

Bibliography

Given the choice of just one book on strategy, it would probably still have to be:

Sloan, A. P. *My years with General Motors* Harmondsworth: Penguin, 1986 (first published 1963)

This has a fair claim to being the best multidisciplinary case study of all time, though it could have been longer; more is needed on competitive strategy towards other producers, for example. And, while the war record is carefully emphasised, little is said on government relations, with nothing at all on the US Trust Department. Today, anyone considering modelling an organisation on the General Motors of 70 years ago might reflect that what was right for 1920 is not necessarily so for 1990. Moreover, Sloan's GM really needed "another Sloan" to run it after his departure in 1956. As it was, the pace of innovation and change slowed after the early 1940s. Much of what later went wrong may be inferred from a careful read of another lengthy book:

Kanter, R. M. *The Change Masters* London: Counterpoint, 1983

Primarily on managing change and innovation, this book nonetheless contains many strategic implications. Above all, it provides a distinctly different concept of how to view and analyse a large corporation for strategic purposes.

Academic cases on strategy come mostly from the United States and are a mixed bag. Four excellent ones from the United Kingdom on Thomas Tilling, Cadbury Schweppes, Manganese Bronze and Tarmac are contained in:

Minkes, A. L. and Nuttall, C. S. *Business Behaviour and Management Structure* Beckenham: Croom Helm, 1985

Biographies of business leaders sell heavily, but all too often cover anecdotal information. They also tend to be, in Peter Drucker's words, of the "Look Ma, no hands!" variety. An exception with an eye for important turning points and critical deals of long ago is:

Kay, W. *Tycoons* London: Piatkus, 1985

A recent exception, with an emphasis on leadership, is:

Harvey-Jones, J. *Making It Happen* London: Collins, 1988

Many books examine success for its lessons, and of these the greatest sale and influence have been achieved by:

Peters, T. J. and Waterman, R. H. *In Search of Excellence* New York: Harper & Row, 1982

This book has been criticised, but it was readable, lively and enthusiastic, and it appeared just after the depth of a recession, when such qualities really were needed. Both authors have since produced what many consider to be better books:

Peters, T. J. *Thriving on Chaos—Handbook for a Management Revolution* London: Macmillan, 1988

Waterman, R. H. *The Renewal Factor* London: Transworld, 1988

Of the other similar works, not solely concerned with strategy, but with very strong strategic implications, try:

O'Toole, J. *Vanguard Management* New York: Doubleday, 1985

And two on Japan:

Abegglen, J. C. and Stalk, G. *Kaisha—The Japanese Corporation* New York: Basic Books, 1985

Ohmae, K. *Triad Power* New York: Free Press, 1985

The last volume departs from the pattern. As well as being based on observation, it is partly the author's vision of the future and partly a public-relations job on Japan for US consumption. The term "Triad" has been widely used in commerce since the book appeared.

Books addressing strategy directly have a different style and often emphasise only a part of the strategic problem. Among the best balanced introductions are:

Karlof, B. *Business Strategy in Practice* Chichester: Wiley, 1987 (first published in Sweden 1985)

Grieve Smith, J. *Business Strategy—An Introduction* Oxford: Blackwell, 1985

Another approach, this time from Switzerland and strong on concentration, is:

Pumpin, C. *The Essence of Corporate Strategy* Aldershot: Gower, 1987

A Japanese contribution, remarkable for its insight and its emphasis on the role of the central strategist, is:

Ohmae, K. *The Mind of the Strategist* New York; McGraw-Hill, 1982 (subsequently issued by Penguin Books Ltd)

This has been criticised as being not quite typical of conditions in Japan, but it should be high on any strategy reading list. Also of compelling merit are Michael Porter's books:

Porter, M. E. *Competitive Strategy* New York: Free Press, 1980

Porter, M. E. *Competitive Advantage* New York: Free Press, 1985

Both works are long, possibly because they set out to make a point and then establish it. If you are interested only in the point, you could start with the summary in the first chapter of *Competitive Advantage* and move on to the value chain. Stakeholders are covered admirably in:

Freeman, R. E. *Strategic Management—A Stakeholder Approach* Marshfield (Mass.): Pitman, 1984

And for a strategic view from the standpoint of leadership try:

Bennis, W. and Nanus, B. *Leaders—The Strategies for Taking Charge* New York: Harper & Row, 1985

The early classics should now be used only with care as practical guides, but they are still of great interest, and Drucker's books wear well. The theory of 20 years ago is demonstrated in:

Ansoff, H. I. *Corporate Strategy* 2nd edition Harmondsworth: Penguin, 1987 (first published 1965)

Drucker, P. E. *The Practice of Management* London: Heinemann, 1955

Drucker, P. E. *Managing for Results* London: Heinemann, 1964

There are several large compilations from the United States of new essays and reprints of some of the best articles down the years. Although these are obviously intended for the US academic market, they are useful for reference over here. A recent example, and probably the best, is:

> Quinn, J. B., Mintzberg, H., and James, R. M. *The Strategy Process* Englewood Cliffs (NJ): Prentice-Hall, 1988

Two critical views of aspects of planning and strategy are cited in the text, but both are likely to be difficult to obtain:

> Quinn, J. B. *Strategies for Change—Logical Incrementalism* Homewood (Ill.): Irwin, 1980

> Thomas, L. G. *The Economics of Strategic Planning* Lexington, Boston: Lexington Books, 1986

Major treatments of corporate planning have the general difficulty that they suggest how the world ought to be rather than describe the way it is. Moreover, views from 15 years ago of what the world ought to look like need not be the same as those which might be expressed today. Examples are:

> Argenti, J. *Systematic Corporate Planning* London: Nelson, 1974

> Hussey, D. E. *Corporate Planning—Theory and Practice* Oxford: Pergamon, 1975

It is recommended that a more recent critical view should be read in conjunction with these, such as the chapters on strategy and planning in:

> Hussey, D. E. *Management Training and Corporate Structures* Oxford: Pergamon, 1988

Marketing is not planning, but in practice most planning comes down to marketing. To develop it, try:

> Christopher, M., Majaro, S., and McDonald, M. *Strategy Search* Aldershot: Gower, 1987

A persuasive case for placing heavy stress on technical change and innovation is made by:

Foster, R. N. *Innovation—The Attacker's Advantage* London: Macmillan, 1986

Six references have been cited for organisational structure:

Burns, T., and Stalker, G. M. *The Management of Innovation* London: Tavistock, 1961

Chandler, A. D. *Strategy and Structure* Cambridge (Mass.): MIT Press, 1962

Fayol, H. *General and Industrial Administration* London: Pitman, 1949 (first published in France 1916)

Lawrence, P. R., and Lorsch, J. W. *Organization and Environment* Homewood (Ill.): Irwin, 1967

Taylor, F. W. *Principles of Scientific Management* New York: Harper, 1911

Woodward, J. *Industrial Organisation—Theory and Practice* Oxford; Oxford University Press, 1965

Rather than go to any of them direct, the reader approaching the subject for the first time is advised to refer to a work covering all of them, such as:

Dessler, G. *Organization Theory* Englewood Cliffs (NJ): Prentice-Hall, 1986

A contrasting view should be taken by referring to one of the British treatments, for example:

Handy, C. B. *Understanding Organisations* 3rd edition Harmondsworth: Penguin, 1985

Kakabadse, A., Ludlow, R., and Vinnicombe, S. *Working in Organisations* Aldershot: Gower, 1977

The questions of how an organisation is run and what the role of the centre should be are raised in:

Goold, M., and Campbell, A. *Strategies and Styles* Oxford: Blackwell, 1987

It is hard to find an effective piece on forecasts suitable for corporate applications. However, those interested in trying to explore the limits of forecasting potential should try:

Makridakis, S., and Wheelwright, S. C. *The Handbook of Forecasting* 2nd edition New York: Wiley, 1987

But this is strictly for reference only. Despite its length, it is weak on financial markets, one of the key areas for strategy.

Deterministic methods are given short shrift in the current book, yet certain tactical decisions are open to a probabilistic approach. Some of the scope here is indicated by:

Schelling, T. C. *The Strategy of Conflict* New York: Oxford University Press, 1963.

Statements such as "von Clausewitz's *On War* is the best book on marketing" or "The best book on strategy is Machiavelli's, *The Prince*" are heard less often than they used to be, but such attitudes are still around. And, of course, autocratic styles, conditioned in any of several ways, are widely seen, especially in smaller businesses. For an introduction, try one of the very few humorous management books to have stood the test of time:

Jay, A. *Management and Machiavelli* London: Hodder & Stoughton, 1970

Finally, there are the four principal references used to research the diamond sector:

Bruton, E. *Diamonds* London: N.A.G., 1970

Epstein, E. J. *The Diamond Invention* London: Hutchinson, 1982

Herbert, I. *The Diamond Diggers* London: Tom Stacey, 1972

Lenzen, G. *The History of Diamond Production and the Diamond Trade* London: Barrie & Jenkins, 1970 (first published in Germany 1966).

Index